LIFE ACCORDING TO
THE RULES OF
BOXING

101 Rules to Being the Champion of Your Own Life

Iser Family 🙂
Elijah & Noah - Be your own
HERO

JOLIE GLASSMAN *of your story!*

BALBOA.PRESS
A DIVISION OF HAY HOUSE

You are it!
Jolie Glassman

Balboa Press books may be ordered through booksellers or by contacting:

Balboa Press
A Division of Hay House
1663 Liberty Drive
Bloomington, IN 47403
www.balboapress.com
844-682-1282

Because of the dynamic nature of the Internet, any web addresses or links contained in this book may have changed since publication and may no longer be valid. The views expressed in this work are solely those of the author and do not necessarily reflect the views of the publisher, and the publisher hereby disclaims any responsibility for them.

The author of this book does not dispense medical advice or prescribe the use of any technique as a form of treatment for physical, emotional, or medical problems without the advice of a physician, either directly or indirectly. The intent of the author is only to offer information of a general nature to help you in your quest for emotional and spiritual well-being. In the event you use any of the information in this book for yourself, which is your constitutional right, the author and the publisher assume no responsibility for your actions.

Cover Photos taken by Magda Hernandez

Print information available on the last page.

ISBN: 978-1-9822-7595-2 (sc)
ISBN: 978-1-9822-7597-6 (hc)
ISBN: 978-1-9822-7596-9 (e)

Library of Congress Control Number: 2021921447

Balboa Press rev. date: 12/15/2021

CONTENTS

Foreword ix

Introduction xi

About This Book xxi

Preface 1

1: Always Chase the Perfect Punch 6

2: Wherever You Go, There You Are 8

3: Believe in Yourself—Confidence Is Key 10

4: Develop the Internal Immunity of Grit 14

5: Willingness to Sacrifice 18

6: Bob and Weave, Stick and Move 20

7: Own Your Power 22

8: The Foundation and Basics Are Everything..............26

9: Commitment to Excellence 28

10: Know Yourself 34

11: Be Strategic 36

12: Dig Deep 38

13: Fight, Think, Learn, and Be Smart 40

14: Don't Be a Follower 42

15: Never Use the Same Timing, Rhythm, or Tempo.................. 44

16: Train to Win..46

17: Be Intentional 48

18: See Everything..50

19: Practice Is Key, and You Can Never Practice Enough 52

20: Be Resilient...54

21: Face Your Fears Head-On 56

22: Believe It, Then You Will See It 58

23: Adjust and Respond Best Under Pressure 60

24: No One Is Coming to Save You 62

25: Self-Control Is Required—Stay Calm 64

26: Nothing Works without Integrity 66

27: Life Is Not Fair: Play Full Out Anyway 70

28: Be Coachable 72

29: Touch Gloves, Honor, Respect 74

30: Hit and Don't Get Hit 76

31: Always Motivate Yourself 78

32: Have Passion—Love What You Do 80

33: Mindset Is Everything 82

34: Don't Get Backed in the Corner, and When You Do,
     Know How to Get Out 84

35: Keep It in the Ring 86

36: Know When to Pivot 88

37: Styles Make Fights 90

38: The People in Your Corner Help Make You a
     Champion or Not 92

39: Don't Be Predictable 94

40: Be First, Be Brave, and Have Courage 96

41: Pray, Have Faith, and Believe in a Higher Power 98

42: Be Positive 100

43: Have Patience 102

44: Never Turn Your Back 104

45: Trust the Process: Surrender 106

46: Dress How You Want to Be Perceived 108

47: Feel—You Need to Mourn 110

48: Timing Is Everything 114

49: Must Be Present at All Times 116

50: Always Be Ready 118

51: Prepare for the Unexpected 120

52: Play Big..122

53: Appreciate—Have Gratitude...............................124

54: Don't Worry About What Others Are Doing.........128

55: Be Vigilant, Keep Your Hands Up, And Protect Yourself
     At All Times 130

56: Balance Is Everything 132

57: Remember Where You Came From, and It Doesn't
     Have to Be Where You're Going 136

58: Find and Create Openings 138

59: Make Yourself Comfortable with the Uncomfortable 140

60: Fight Your Heart Out—Boxers Are All Heart......144

61: Be an Amazing Problem Solver 146

62: Show No Pain..150

63: Fight to Your Strengths: Use Your Assets, Your Best Tools 152

64: Always Have a Plan and Back-Up Plans as Well..........154

65: Don't Lose Focus: Keep Your Eyes on the Target 156

66: Refuse To Lose 158

67: Learn Who Your Real Friends Are 160

68: Be Super Disciplined and Dedicated 162

69: When People Tell You That You Can't Do It, Prove
     Them Wrong...164

70: Never Give Up..168

71: Be in Flow 170

72: Leave It All in the Ring—Give It Your All...........172

73: You Will Become Humble 174

74: Be Precise...176

75: Experience Mostly Wins 178

76: You Will Learn How Strong You Really Are 180

77: Temptation Is A Real Thing...............................182

78: Don't Show Weaknesses...184

79: Pain and Suffering Are Part of It............................186

80: How You Train Is How You Fight........................188

81: Don't Take Unnecessary Punishment...................190

82: Roll with the Punches...192

83: Fight When You Don't Want to Fight...............194

84: Come Out Winning..196

85: Don't Underestimate Your Opponents, and Don't
   Overestimate Them Either....................................198

86: Stay Active, Keep Moving, Never Stop............... 200

87: Study Your Competition, Outwit Your Opponents, and
   Create Leverage...202

88: Be Proud of Yourself—Celebrate Your Wins....... 204

89: Inspire Others to Be Great—Serve......................206

90: Hire and Have a Coach..210

91: Sometimes the Towel Needs to Be Thrown In....212

92: Every Punch Sets Up the Next—Generate Power.................214

93: Control Your Breathing: Self-Regulate.................216

94: Always Be in Shape and Super Fit and Lean..........................220

95: There Are No Shortcuts to Success.......................222

96: Recovery Is a Daily Must......................................224

97: Health and Diet Are of Top Priority....................226

98: Take Responsibility..236

99: Finish Strong..240

100: Be Reflective—Evaluate..242

101: Leave a Legacy..246

Conclusion...249

About the Author...267

FOREWORD

I'd like to say this is an outstanding young woman who knows the preparations required for fitness and for calculating good health and good food. Many, many people have come to her famous gym to visit, film, celebrate, and train—greats such as Muhammad Ali, Angelo Dundee, Evander Holyfield, Roy Jones Jr., Bernard Hopkins, Lennox Lewis, Chris Bosch, Will Smith, and many, many others. I offer a tribute to this woman, who is an amazing person who has transformed the lives of tens of thousands of people throughout her thirty-plus years of in-depth experience in fitness, health and wellness, business, education, transformation, inspiration, and leadership. She has her own 501(c)3 called Jolie's Kids, and she helps society and the community by assisting children and families in working out and doing healthy things in this world. Jolie is the queen and the owner of this world-famous South Beach Boxing gym. She is loved, honored, respected, and admired, *and* I like to call her my daughter. I am so proud of her, all of her hard work, and the lifelong career of experiences that went into writing this book. I know it's going to be a game changer for teens and adults, both women and men. Jolie is all about making an impact and transforming lives.

—Khalilah Camacho-Ali,
former wife of Muhammad Ali and mother to their four children

INTRODUCTION

My primary goal in life is to transform people's lives on the greatest scale possible with grace and ease. I have been studying personal development for thirty-plus years, solid and hard. I am a super overachiever. Everything I do is stronger, better, fitter, faster, and longer, always. There are many things I do not want to do, but I do them because I said I would. People often need a breakdown to have a breakthrough, so I drive myself into breakdown and get breakthroughs because, if I am committed to transforming the world, I must transform myself. So I am always hitting walls and going through them. I live to serve. I want to find every space and every opportunity to make a difference, always be serving, always be contributing, and always be adding to people's lives. When you stand for someone and their transformation, it becomes easy because you are standing for them. All that matters is serving.

I always tell people, "Boxing is life." Boxers go through struggles and must have commitment and discipline when they fight as they're not only dealing with each opponent; they are also dealing with themselves, consistently and always. My philosophy of fitness and life is that it is the moments between the notes that create the music. It is all about getting to the space in between, and that is the essence of boxers' workouts. Boxers create moments and movements, and every punch sets up the next, just like in life. Everything you do sets up the next thing. Everything you are doing is having an effect on everything else. I love sharing with people consistency and dedication and helping them get what they want and beat the voices in their heads.

It is about being the winner of yourself and honoring yourself, going when you do not want to go, doing what you said you would do, and being your word. Because how you do one thing is how you do everything. So when you really get strong, you take on your whole life strong. Do what you do best, do what you love, and stay in action, and the universe will hook you up.

I am a professionally certified life coach with several degrees, licenses, and certifications in the education, behavior, self-improvement, and personal development arenas. I specialize in health and wellness, sports and fitness, transition and loss, relationship issues, family issues, and business issues. I motivate, train, and teach people; get them into action; and then hold them accountable so they can love the lives they live and live the lives they love.

I am also a fitness and wellness coach. I motivate people to live healthy, active, and balanced lifestyles that bring balance, strength, flexibility, focus, and discipline to their minds, bodies, and spirits.

I am your tow truck when you get stuck in the mud of life.

You can lead a horse to water; it's *my job to make 'em thirsty.*

Are you living your purpose, on purpose, purposely?

My name is Jolie Glassman, and for the past thirty-plus years, I have led people to generate lives greater than they ever knew they could be. I do *intervention* and *integration therapy*. I help you with yourself, your kids, and others, leading you to create and live a life you want and love, filled with honor, peace, vitality, and full self-expression. My promise is that you will be better, stronger, fitter, and more connected mentally, emotionally, physically, and spiritually. You will be ready to take on your life in a whole new way that produces the results you only ever dreamed about, and you will be touched, loved, and inspired.

You will be proud of who you are!

> *I learn so I can teach.*
> *I share so I can transform.*
> *I serve so I can live in joy.*

I transform and inspire others to become strong, courageous, fit, healthy, and happy. I show people how great they are.

I am a boxer, *in life*.

Throughout my life I have had to fight to get to where I am. I am the product of an old, famous, rich man and a young, hot woman. My parents were thirty-one years apart in age, and my dad was Judy Garland's producer, among other amazing things. I was born in Beverly Hills, California, the youngest of three sisters. My father passed away when I was two years old, and we moved to New York. When I was seven years old, we moved to South Florida so my mom could be closer to family—well, her sister and her sister's kids. My mom raised us three girls on her own, and she was extremely strict with manners, our education, and dating. We had to get straight A's in school. She was not around much, as she worked through the nights making chocolate novelties and slept in through the late morning, so I always say I raised myself. I started doing my own projects and homework and making my own breakfasts and lunches in kindergarten. The fear of her screaming and losing her temper, and her crazy and lengthy punishments, would keep me in line and overachieving immensely. I also knew I wanted to do well in life and not struggle as she did. Living at home with my mom was very tumultuous and inconsistent, and I wanted to get out of the house and live on my own as soon as possible.

When I was a little girl in early elementary school, I was terrible in physical education class. Last one around the track had to run it again, and it was always me. I was a bit mouthy, and I would speak up, screaming out across the field, "Why would the person who is the worst have to do it again? That makes no sense!" It was so embarrassing that I made a decision to never be last again. From then on, I pushed myself hard in physical education, and by fifteen years old, I was in the gyms religiously. I was already an A student and graduated top of my class, and then I was getting better in fitness and strength. It affected all areas of my life. I loved it. It became my life. I remember being so mesmerized by the beautiful, older women who were strong and extremely fit. I knew I wanted to be like them. The vision I made up of them was what I strived to be. Being strong was always appealing to me, and I knew I wanted to chase it as I did not want to be weak—and if I was not strong, I was weak. Thank God, as it gave me the energy, know-how, and focus to fight and follow my heart. You cannot have a strong mind and a strong life with a weak body. In everything I did, I chased strength and avoided weak. I knew I wanted to be strong in all areas.

Areas in which I Had to Fight Hard

I grew up with a single mother and two older sisters. My mother was bipolar, extremely strict, and often physically and verbally abusive. I am not sure a day went by that my mom was not screaming and yelling at us that we would end up in the streets and homeless. She would scream about how she could not afford to pay the bills, yet she shopped religiously and had overly expensive taste. I ran away at sixteen, almost seventeen, years old and put myself through college. My mom even made it harder for me to accomplish this by not giving me her tax returns to prove she did not even claim me as a dependent. I had to get emancipated in the courts to qualify for financial aid of any sort.

I do know my mom did the best she could, but she was obviously not prepared, or mentally equipped, to raise three young children on her own without their father and a husband. Even though I grew up in a lot of chaos and came from a great amount of adversity, I am eternally grateful to her, as she did instill great morals and values in us girls. I would not be the woman I am today if she were not the mother she was.

More ways I had to fight include the many interactions with medications prescribed for me for various reasons from the time I was a young teenager throughout my midtwenties. For bad skin and breakouts, a doctor gave me tetracycline by the hundreds to be taken twice daily. For bad menstrual cycles, a doctor prescribed birth control pills, which ended up having lots of side effects. Then, when I was an older teenager, my gynecologist prescribed me the antidepressant Paxil for moodiness. I wanted to commit suicide when I tried to get off it. I had to wean myself down to a crumb of a tiny pill just to ensure I could make it through the day without wanting to kill myself. Later, in my early twenties I went to an ear, nose, and throat doctor because I was sick and had a sore throat. Plus I knew that I had never learned to speak right, as I spoke from my chest and did not take full breaths. The doctor prescribed me Nexium, "the purple pill," as it was called on a popular television commercial. But I researched natural remedies and cured it on my own, without ever taking that purple pill. It's no wonder we see acid reflux medications at the front counter in every drugstore.

Then there was allergy medicine all over the place and flu medicine as well, until now. Do they even talk about the flu anymore?

In 1997, I became a schoolteacher after graduating from a scholarship program called FOCUS, For Our Children in Urban Settings. I graduated at the top of my class with a bachelor's in education, a master's in behavior modification, and minors in art history, religion, and philosophy. I taught school in only the inner cities at first and then in alternative education units, detention centers, and jails. I taught elementary education and then middle and high school English and language arts. I worked with only the so-called problem children, as they were my specialty, and then I also worked with emotionally handicapped and severely emotionally disturbed students for a short time. Teaching in these schools was always a fight for me as I dealt with reverse discrimination and "the system." I would fight for the kids, and nothing got in my way of my mission to disrupt education the way it was, to be a changemaker, and to transform lives. I lived for those kids. I was teaching boxing all along without even really knowing what the sport was about, yet I knew how to manage my class and make everyone feel and know they were included. I would never tolerate bullying, but when my kids wanted to fight, I would allow it and facilitate it. I would move all the chairs to open up a space for them to fight. The rules were that I needed to know about it beforehand and that no one else could jump in; it was one-on-one only. It was amazing to see the instantaneous results and to control the bullying and fighting, create community, and provide a space that truly facilitated fun and learning. I was constantly fighting when I was a teacher—fighting for the kids' rights, fighting for better teachers, fighting for the system to be run better, fighting the labels and medications that kids were given unnecessarily, and fighting what was being taught instead of a recipe for being successful in life. Essentially, in my opinion, our public schools misallocate funds, teach kids how to waste time, and often do stupid things in stupid ways.

In the end of 2001, I quit teaching to run our gyms and open more locations. That was a fight as well since I did not want to quit what was my calling in life. But it was serendipitous and no mistake that I got into boxing. I went on to own boxing gyms for over twenty years and developed a charity program called Jolie's Kids. Our slogan is "We teach kids to fight so they don't. It takes a village; *we are the village.*" Our kids are our future. I always say how our young people do not pass through an "adult archway" at eighteen years old. They need to be taught useful knowledge, how-to's, critical thinking, coping skills, life skills, communication skills, business development, and successful habits from a very young age. I am grateful that I got to meld it all together—teaching, boxing, fitness, community, and wellness. I am also grateful for being a fighter in life as it is a beautiful thing to stay in action, always do what you love, travel the world, honor yourself while being fully self-expressed, and serve the world as an extension of who you are authentically, knowing that God is in charge and has a bigger plan for you. I always say that God is like the rose-petal thrower in a wedding. God does not place the rose petal down until you are right there, ready to step up to it. We need to stay in action, always do the next right thing, and trust the process. Believe in the memories of your created future more than the half-memorized memories of your past. Follow and embody all these 101 rules and know that *everything is always working out for you, and it will.*

In late 2007, during the terrible economic recession, I got a divorce after ten years of marriage. It was very costly and ugly and went on for over three years. This was my biggest fight and my biggest accomplishment, as I committed to remaining conscious throughout the whole ordeal, including all the nastiness. I knew that doing the right thing and following my heart would take me to where I needed to be. I lead from my heart, so when something does not *feel* right or good, I do not do it. My spouse and I had owned three gyms together, and after the three years of nasty fighting and shadiness, I got back my South Beach Boxing gym location in South Beach. However, I also had several hundred thousand dollars in debt to deal with, as well as people attempting to buy the gym from underneath me. They could not do so, thankfully, as I had filed an injunction in the courts which protected me from the gym being sold from underneath me.

On Valentine's Day 2010, exactly twelve years to the day after I had gotten married, I officially got my gym back. Of course, it required a fight, as boxing is a corrupt and dirty sport; of course, there was shadiness involved, yet I would rather focus on what I am creating versus what I could destroy. I do not worry about the competition because there is enough for all, and when you serve and live authentically as your truest and highest self, cocreate and surrender to the process, and let God lead the way, all works out and good prevails. I love the mantra, "Everything is *always* working out for me." Do good things and good things come back to you. Always come from a place of love.

I am clear that I am a fighter, yet I pick my battles and fight from love. I fight for that which is worth fighting for, and I build my team. During the three-plus years of my divorce, I was immersed in Landmark Education, a personal development program about living powerfully and producing great results in your life. I led introductions in people's homes, following the pathway to becoming a Landmark Forum leader. When I knew I was getting my baby back, my gym, I was a bit torn as I had been planning and was prepared to give up my life to lead the Landmark Forum around the world. Then, one of my best friends, April, told me, "You can still be what a 'Landmark Forum Leader,' is, an unwavering stand for transformation, yet as the gym owner of South Beach Boxing." Duh! She was right, and there went my journey of building my house of transformation.

Life is a constant fight. In 2011, I got into a motorcycle accident that herniated eleven discs and split my head open. I was told I needed ankle surgery, epidurals, and immediate spinal fusion surgery. Many years have passed since then, and I am on a forever journey of healing naturally through many different modalities, as I have been doing it without the use of medications or having any surgeries.

Those are just some of the battles I have had to fight. As Jim Rohn said, "Don't wish things were easier; wish you were better." Things are not easy, yet you can always get better. The keys are to know who you are, know what you want, know what you stand for, always create the win-win, ask for what you want, and fight from a place of love and honor. You have to fight for what you believe in, for what is right, and for a better life. Everybody fights, so what are you fighting for? Always come from a place of love, follow the joy, and live in wellness.

Make smart choices, think smart, reflect on everything, have integrity, communicate clearly and fully, and take responsibility for everything that shows up for you and your life, as then you are just able to respond. Relax and respond only when necessary; otherwise, relax and surrender. "Float like a butterfly and sting like a bee." *Be like a boxer*—bob and weave, stick and move, and get through the eye of the needle. Stay calm in the storms. See everything, have divergent focus, open your awareness, and be aware constantly. Work harder on yourself than you do on anything else, and life will become easier. *Fight! Play to win*! Nobody is getting out alive; play full out. This is not a dress rehearsal; it is your one and only chance at a life. Do not dream your life; live your dream. Live a created life.

Humans have an innate need to be winners because winners belong. Winners reap the benefits and rewards in life. If you hold the trophy or the belt, you hold the power and the status of achievement. You earn your championship in practice as champions are made when nobody is watching. Sports mirror life, and wherever you go, there you are. Success is not a destination; it is earned every day. I always say, "the hardest thing in life is 'easier said than done.'" To be a champion, you need talent, skill, and hard work, yet hard work beats talent when talent does not work. Your success lies in your choices, and the magic of it is created in the process, not the outcome. The destination is the journey. I have a sign over my bed that says, "It's the journey; enjoy the process." It is the everyday, small choices that challenge your comfort zones and complacency. Small choices have us embrace accountability, build grit, and create life-changing results when made consistently over time. We do not wish for success; we work for it. Our greatest opponent is the one we see in the mirror every day. The only relationship that needs working on is the one with yourself, and then if you always bring your best self and come from a place of love, you can be truly present and aligned with your greatest self as well as *bob and weave* most effectively through life. The quality of our lives equals the quality of communication we have with ourselves first and then the world around us. Be the energy you want to attract. People who are in love with themselves will find love in others. Self-discovery and self-mastery are what life is all about.

Be FIT—fight for intentional transformation, from a place of love. Contribute to society, make an impact, honor yourself, take care of yourself, serve, and follow all these 101 rules to be *the champion boxer of your own life. Be the undisputed champ, the hero you have always been waiting for—you are it. Be your future self now!*

Each chapter will identify and detail a different rule and trait you must possess to ensure that you are the hero of your own life. Each rule is paired with a famous boxer's quote or two. The traits discussed are what champion boxers possess. They are what successful people who win at life possess. These traits are results not of genetics but of key choices made on a daily basis. They are simple yet not easy. If they were easy, everyone would be a champion. Just know you have what it takes to be the champion of your own story. My intention is that this book will be the catalyst that opens your eyes to the choices champions make while inspiring you to do the same. This is a curriculum for living a powerful and successful life you love.

Be a champion. You've got what it takes.

ABOUT THIS BOOK

All of us fight. We fight for the things we believe in. We also fight for those we love, and at times we need to fight against our toughest opponent—ourselves, including our minds, thoughts, beliefs, stories, and voices in our heads.

This book is a curriculum for how to live a powerful and successful life you love. It is about how to live your life like a boxer and be the champion fighter of your own life. You are the hero you have been waiting for; it is your future self.

Be your future self now. Become stronger, fitter, faster, better, and wiser in mind, body, and spirit—and all in good fun!

This is truly a book about chasing mastery, being successful and at the top of your game, and being the champion of your own life. It is a boxer's journey, being a fighter in life. It's the journey of a hero that helps you be your future self, the hero you have been waiting for. You are the hero. So you are living the life of a hero; *you* are the main character of your story. Be your own hero. What drives you is your *desire*. Where are you going, what are you working toward, and why do you do what you do? You have what you want, and then there is what you need. Whenever we make plans in life, we bump into opponents. Some are external and others are internal, but it is the internal opponents that get us the most. Inside every single one of us is a strength that is greater than the fear and the sadness, and in any moment you can change your situation and beat the voice in your head. If you do not like where you are, change it. I did not say it would be easy, but it will be worth it. To have a foreground you need a background, as it is all about the contrast. Life exists in polarity and in the midst of contrast. Life is about moments and the spaces in between them. Beating yourself up will not make things better, not one ounce. Energy is life, and when you beat yourself up you lose your energy; therefore, you lose your life. Every person's life story is either a warning or an example. The story we tell ourselves is how we perceive the world. Change your story change your life, and *be the example,* not the warning. Emotion is energy in motion. Feel great emotions, exemplify greatness, and exist in flow.

Be the winner of your own story, your own (created) life. You are the hero you have been waiting for. Chase your best self. Be your future self *now*!

In your head, make the winning voice the one in charge of the committee. Have a strong command voice that moves you into action consistently and always. Say, "I am doing it now." And then do it now! Create the *now* habit, not the *later* habit, as sometimes *later* becomes *never.*

Be the champion fighter of your own life. Be your own champion. Fight! Box!

This is how I take a stand with the committee in my head: My mind says, *I don't want to do it. I'm going to die. I so don't feel like doing this.* And then I reply, "I'm doing it now!"

Interject and intervene. Decide! Commit! Act! Win! Repeat!

Mel Robbins has the "Five Second Rule," which is awesome. Find your rule.

What is your pattern to success? Make it a successful one that produces the most desirable results. If you really want something and you really mean it, do it! Prove it to yourself! Be the hero in your own life. Win! Plan to win! Do what it takes to win! Have it all!

Don't have *either-or* conversations. Know you can have it all and live the life you always dreamed. Only you can do it. It's your life! Go on and live a life you love.

Live fully, powerfully, and effectively, with joy and fulfillment, all while being fully self-expressed. Let me continue to take you on this journey and show you how great you are.

Adopt these 101 rules. You will get all the juice out of life. Live! Have it all. Wish for it, and plan for it. Work for it! Do what it takes. Follow the recipes. Use the correct ingredients if you want your life to be extra delicious—scrumdittliumptious.

Do not die with your music still in you. Embrace silence. Surrender. Be fully self-expressed.

PREFACE

Who I Am

I am a fighter. I am a boxer in life. I started, owned, and operated the world-famous boxing gym, South Beach Boxing in 1998. It was the rebirth of the original 5th Street Gym that closed its doors for good in 1993 when the building was condemned, and we opened two blocks down on the same side of the street in a similar, upstairs, old-school location just five years later. We had all the most famous boxers, professional athletes, singers, and actors frequent our gym—people such as Muhammad Ali, Beau Jack, Roberto Duran, all the Camachos, Lennox Lewis, Roy Jones Jr., Floyd Mayweather Jr., Bernard Hopkins, Mike Tyson, Evander Holyfield, Chris Bosch, Will Smith, and Matt Damon, just to name a few. Boxing has been my life since 1998, yet I come from a teaching and behavioral, educational background. For over thirty years, I have transformed and inspired tens of thousands of people to become strong, courageous, empowered, confident, fit, healthy, and happy. I show people how great they are, and together with my amazing teams, we *prove* how great they are and how they can always have everything they want and ask for. They just need to take the necessary actions that take them down those desired pathways.

Throughout my life, I have always had to fight for what I wanted, for my dreams, my visions, my discipline, and my honor. I always fought for what I believed in my heart, for what was right, and I always fought for the underdog. My academic background is in education and behavior, and I have been a student of life for over thirty solid years. I have spent well over a million dollars on self-improvement, personal development, behavioral sciences, and continued education. I have always lived by the motto from Jim Rohn, "Work harder on yourself than you do on your job and life becomes easier." I live to serve and transform lives. Because

1

of my mission, I have had to also transform myself over and over to be the path to inspiration and transformation in others.

Prior to owning my second boxing gym, as there were three, I was a schoolteacher, and I taught the alternative education units. I always favored the so-called bad or problem kids. My passion and talent for teaching them led me to teach in detention centers and lockdown facilities. I was "teaching boxing" before I even knew what boxing was. I was this thin, young girl with long, blond hair who taught in only the inner cities. I taught in the worst of the worst, and I had a reputation for being able to keep the kids in order and producing great results. Others always asked me how I did it and what my secret was.

The secret is that I am kind, nice, and loving. I listen and honor others without judgments. If the kids wanted to fight, I would allow it, but my rule was that it could be one on one only. No one else could jump into the fight. One of my top strengths is being an *includer* and I do not tolerate bullying. I would move the chairs and desks and let just the two kids fight. It was amazing how, instantaneously, the kids would stop ganging up on one another and would settle down with respect. Consistency was of the utmost importance, along with great manners and respect. Fun was also important, and they knew not to mistake my kindness for weakness.

I am the energy of my boxing gyms. I am a transformation and life-alignment expert. I am in the business of making people feel, look, and *be* outstanding in all areas of their lives they wish to be. I live to make an impact and a difference in every moment and in every interaction. I look to create a win-win outcome and to be, and spread, amazing energy that others then spread like wildfire. I show people how great they are and facilitate environments of pure, magical energy. My mission statement at my gym is, "We build fit, confident, strong, powerful, healthy minds and bodies and infect you with insane, happy, fun energy." If you walk into a boxing gym you will see rich mixing with the poor, young mixing with the older, different races mixing together, and no false pretenses— just love and unity. The world would be a better place if it were more like a boxing gym.

2

Why I've Written This Book and Who It Is For

In a world of information, ignorance is a choice. We are in a time where everyone needs to do their own research, be smart, and learn how to do whatever it is they need to do to get to where they want to go. We all make our own choices, but we need to make much more informed and well-thought-out choices. We must gain knowledge and experiences and learn from them all to live extraordinary lives. Everyone needs to fight from a place of love. We can always create a win-win outcome, honor ourselves, be fully self-expressed, and own our own power; we just need to bring our best selves forward—nothing less. We need to lead from our hearts. We need to fight for what we believe in and gather all the skills we can throughout life to become the greatest version of ourselves. It all begins with self-love and self-care. Self-care is our superpower. We all need to be boxers in life, which is why I wrote this book—to give you all the traits and skills needed to become your greatest self and the champion fighter of your own life. The shortest distance between two points is a straight line, and this book is your straight line to becoming the hero you have been waiting for. The *hero is you.*

It's funny how often people would congratulate me on writing a book and I did not think it was such a big deal. But then I got into the middle of it and was trying to finish it, so when people congratulated me, I thought, *Damn right.* Writing a book, for me, was no joke. Whenever I reserved time for my writing, I often was not inspired, and then I was often inspired when I did not have the time. I had to use my own rules to push through, not quit, and remember why I started to write this in the first place. I live by these rules. I constantly remind myself of them and practice daily. They are not a destination; they are a way of life. They are the journey. Life is lived in the moment and generated moment by moment. All these rules are tools to keep in your toolbox. They are your weapons for winning in life. Since I live to transform lives, am a disruptor for education, and am always looking to make an impact, I wanted to create a book to use as a teaching tool and a curriculum for people to learn and obtain the *real* skills that matter most in life. My whole brand was always about a real gym, real people, and real results, and I am known as a real-talk, straight-shooting teacher, coach, and mentor. I figured it was time to get *real* in the world, not have anything sugar coated, and identify all the necessary tools and skills needed to be a winner and the champion of your own life. A new world is needed, and we need you to cocreate this new world.

This book is not for sissies; underachievers; or those not seeking growth, success, and achievement. I love the metaphor of boxing in life. The same rules a boxer follows to become a champion are those we all need to follow to become champions in our own lives. This book is for those who want to have lives that work in their own favor and who want to always strive for greatness and chase mastery. It is for those who want to box in life and be the champion fighters in their own stories. I wrote this book for kids and adults, both male and female. This book is for winners and those who want to reap the benefits and rewards in life.

Be the hero you have been waiting for. You are it! You are born alone, you die alone, but you are never alone. We are all in our own worlds, in one world. Create your own world, and together let us create the world we live in together. We collectively create it, whether it is conscious or not. Let us do it consciously.

Live life like a boxer. Follow and live by these 101 rules.

Stay tuned for the *Life According to the Rules of Boxing* companion book, which will put you to work and get you in action to become the champion of your own life. It will be released shortly after this one so you can integrate these rules into your life via the critical thinking questions asked for each rule and an accompanying journal to take notes, write answers, and reflect. Fulfillment comes from wrestling with the great questions of life. The answers are in the questions. I will provide the great questions, and you will come up with all the answers needed to take your life to champion status.

How to Read This Book

Live life like a boxer if you want to lead the life of a champion, hero, or legend.

There are 101 rules. You can skip around or just open to any rule and read it. They are in no particular order, and they are all equally important for the most part. *Everything is important, and nothing does not matter,* like phonics and whole language—you need them both. You need the breakdown of the whole, and you need the whole in operation. Read them all, and then read one a day or however often to be inspired and "close the distance," like a boxer does, from where you are to where you want to be. To live life like a boxer who trains to be a champion and becomes one, follow, learn, and embody the rules. You for sure have what it takes. Know this, and then do what it takes.

All rules are paired with a quote or two from a famous boxer or boxing trainer. Collectively, the rules say it all. Many I do not even have to elaborate on, even though I do, so just let it sit; *be with the rule* and reflect on whether you currently possess this skill or trait. If not, think about how exactly you will begin to incorporate it into your life and embody it. Write all over in this book. Make it your Bible for success. Highlight what stands out to you most and write all in the margins. Fold pages and come back to those that inspire you most. Read these often and heed them regularly. *Allow me to transform your life and show you how great you are.*

Again, stay tuned for my next book, the companion journal of questions to these 101 rules.

Know that every time I refer to a *boxer* in this book, I am not speaking of just any boxer. I am speaking of those who are on the track to becoming champions or are already champions. There is "great" and "not great" in all areas of life, including sports. These 101 rules are for becoming the *very best,* a *champion,* the *champion of your own life.*

Many concepts are repeated in different ways and in new contexts, so listen to them and hear them anew. Keep this book nearby, whether on your coffee table, next to your toilet, or on your bedside table, and read it over and over again to create a creative, powerful, inspired, fulfilled, and ultrasuccessful life.

#1
ALWAYS CHASE THE
PERFECT PUNCH

I fight for perfection. Never achieve it, no one does,
but we aim for it.
— Mike Tyson

This is truly a book about chasing mastery. It is a boxer's journey, being a fighter in life. Mastery does not mean you are the best in the world; it means you are on your path to explore how to be your best. Mastery of self heading toward the mastery of your craft is the pathway. No matter how much you work on perfecting your craft, there is always more to get to, another level to achieve. You never get there, as the destination is the journey, and you never truly master a craft, as you are always chasing that perfect punch. Mike Tyson says he aims for perfection and knows he never achieves it, yet he keeps fighting for it. I often tell people who are new to boxing and want to begin training that there are six different punches that take a lifetime to learn. You are consistently working on perfecting the basics. Boxing is constantly a challenge. It forevermore has one up on you, so there is always more to strive for and more improvements to make just like in life. That is the beauty of it. It never gets any easier; you just get better. Always strive to be the best and

Chase the perfect punch.

#2
WHEREVER YOU GO,
THERE YOU ARE

To see a man beaten not by a better opponent but
by himself is a tragedy.
— Cus D'Amato

One of my favorite things I often say is, "We are all in our own world, in one world." We create our own realities. We are the primary characters in the stories we tell as our lives. The lives we live and all the ways that we interpret what we see are just our perceptions and projections. Most of the time we don't interact with people, we interact with our own thoughts. The person you think you are does not even exist outside your mind. Like Wayne Dyer said, "When you change the way you look at things, the things you look at change." Everything we look at is defined by our stories, perceptions, views, and beliefs, and all of these elements are drawn from the past. Emotions are products of past experiences; therefore, everywhere we go, we bring our pasts with us. That is why the primary obstacle in the way of people's success is themselves. We are always in our own way when we are not in flow and not moving graciously toward our most desirable, highest selves.

The key is to always notice who you are being and to remember that wherever you go, there you are. Face yourself head-on, just like boxers do. Boxers are very clear that every time they step in the ring, they are fighting themselves. They know that their greatest opponent is themselves. All of us fight. We fight for things we believe in and for those we love, but at times we must fight against our greatest opponent: ourselves. When Will Smith trained at my gym for the Ali movie, he told me, "The keys to life are running and reading. Reading because knowledge is power, and running to beat the voice in your head." He told me that he knew he would always be the last one to get off the treadmill as he beats that voice in his head.

You are not what you notice, but you are the noticer of what you notice. Become aware. It is always you. You are the one you have been waiting for. When I was heavily involved in my Landmark Education studies, we would always say, "Nobody is over there." We would snap out of the trance we were in, as it is true: nobody is over there. It is just us and our perceptions. In life, it is not what happens that matters; it is our reactions to things and what we make them mean.

Wherever you go, there you are.

#3
BELIEVE IN YOURSELF—
CONFIDENCE IS KEY

Confidence breeds success and success breeds confidence.
Confidence applied properly surpasses genius.
— Mike Tyson

You can't win without confidence. If my mind can conceive
it, if my heart can believe it—then I can achieve it.
— Muhammad Ali

What we think and what we believe determine the quality of our lives. The beliefs we have about who we are, our "I am" beliefs, are the ones that really shape our lives and are the strongest.

Self-belief is how confident we are in our own skills, behaviors, and abilities. Self-belief is needed in sports performance, especially in boxing, where it is one against one. You cannot win without self-belief. Boxers believe in themselves when no one else does. They do not care what others think. They keep believing in themselves and pushing forward and through as they build their dreams to fruition. Mike Tyson says, "We are a lot stronger than we anticipate we are. We are a lot stronger than we think we are. By believing in yourself you can overcome some of the darkest moments."

Self-confidence is feeling good about yourself. Do your best, and at the end of those days when you feel good about yourself, self-confidence grows. Self-confidence comes from lack of neglect. Honoring yourself, being healthy, and being willing to do whatever it takes develops unbelievable self-confidence. Rise above your circumstances. You got this.

Beliefs create, and beliefs destroy. They control and rule our lives. Beliefs are only thoughts we tell ourselves over and over again, so we are just convinced they are true. A belief is not a truth; it is a feeling of certainty. Catch yourself in the moment of a disempowering belief and replace the old belief with a new, reframed, more empowering belief, constantly, over and over again. Put a different part of you in charge, a more empowering version of you. Start to tell your story and then interject loud and strong and say, "No! What I really mean to say—my new belief and story—is ..." Break the old pattern. You need to catch the pattern the second before it starts, *knock it out,* and replace it with what you would rather believe instead. Then you can align your actions and behaviors with that new belief.

Pay attention. Notice the observer. Become aware of the conversations going on in your head. Humans are meaning-making machines. You do not have to believe everything you think, and if you are going to believe in anything, believe in *yourself.* Take charge and know that you can choose your thoughts, as you do anyhow, and replace the unwanted ones with wanted ones. You just need to slow down enough to notice the programming in your head that runs your life. Don't speak negatively about yourself, even as a joke. Your body doesn't know the difference. Words are energy and cast spells, that's why it's called *spelling*. If you are going to apply yourself to something and want something great for your future and your life, then you need to change out the negative banter in your head for positive talk. Make that change and you will believe it; you don't have to wait until you see it.

Practice daily. Use mantras that make you feel great and say affirmations that affirm your amazing feelings. Have a strong command voice that empowers you to honor yourself and take action, and then prove yourself and believe in yourself. Affirmations without discipline are delusions, so stay disciplined. Say what you want to believe and do what it takes to manifest that belief. You need self-belief to chase your own greatness.

Believe in yourself. Confidence is key.

JOLIE
G
GLASSMAN

#4
DEVELOP THE INTERNAL
IMMUNITY OF GRIT

There are three things you need to remember in boxing:
work hard, work harder, work hardest.
— Manny Paquiao

Develop unshakable grit. Push yourself always. Get used to hard work and nonstop dedication led with passion. Boxers have an insane amount of grit.

Boxers know that when they are not working on perfecting their craft, others are working on perfecting their own crafts to kick their asses. If you want to play with the big dogs, compete at a high level, and be recognized as one of the best, you better develop an internal immunity of grit.

I write this book for this purpose: to inspire you to be the champion boxer of your own life. Being a boxer in life—truly my entire life, even before I owned my boxing gyms—I always possessed grit. I always wanted to overachieve. It was needed to get to where I am. I was teaching in the inner cities, jails, detention centers, and lockdown facilities. Then I became immersed in the world of boxing. I have been involved in the professional sport and worked with professional athletes for over twenty-five years, and I have owned gyms for over twenty-three years, which all required an insane amount of grit. I prevailed through the 2001 terrorist attacks, the 2008 economic and housing market crashes, a messy divorce, and then the 2020 shutdowns due to COVID-19 and that whole economic and governmental fiasco. My gym is in one of the most popular tourist meccas of the world, South Beach, Florida, so we sure did feel the impacts. Grit was needed through all of it.

Grit is the driver of achievement and success. It is a mixture of courage, perseverance, and resilience in the face of setbacks. Grit requires passion, consistency, and the ability to learn from criticism. Developing the internal immunity of grit builds character. Goals are set and then followed through to fruition.

Boxers who become champions have talent and grit. Boxers who do not become champions, yet are bred to be, are missing something in one of those areas. Without grit, talent may be nothing more than unmet potential. A fighter with more grit can beat a fighter with more talent, especially when the talented fighter lacks grit.

The great news is that grit is not an inherited trait; it is a learned behavior. Find your passion and develop an internal immunity of grit to chase your dreams and whatever sets your soul on fire.

Meditate with the vision and those feelings. Make your internal experiences stronger and more vivid than any other memories of past experiences and then act accordingly to cocreate and allow all your imagined dreams and visions to come true. Be the hardest worker in the room, and lead by example. Hard work does pay off.

Develop the internal immunity of grit.

#5
WILLINGNESS TO SACRIFICE

I'm willing to do anything to myself to improve to be the best. I'm willing to sacrifice my body, my psychological health, to just be the best in the world. That's what sacrifice is; you really have to sacrifice your life. I do what others are not willing to do. When you have something in life that you want to accomplish greatly, you have to be willing to give up your happiness.
— Mike Tyson

Chasing mastery; becoming a champion; competing with the big dogs; being the hero of your own life; looking back without regrets; and obtaining a feeling of success, fulfillment, and satisfaction all require a willingness to sacrifice. It will hurt. It will take time. It will require dedication and willpower. You will need to make healthy decisions. It all requires sacrifice; therefore, you can either resist it and constantly bang up against it or just go with it because you want the results. It is a much more positive and empowering connotation.

Mike Tyson told me one day that he wakes up at 2:00 a.m. and will train and run in a blizzard because he knows no one else will. As he says, the others would just get on a treadmill instead. Being willing to do what no one else will do is how winning happens. You will need to push your body to its maximum and never give up. There will be temptation, there will be adversity, there will be setbacks, and there will be bad days and good days. But I promise you this—when you reach your goal, it will have been worth it. Just

Be willing to sacrifice.

#6
BOB AND WEAVE,
STICK AND MOVE

Life doesn't run away from nobody. Life runs at people.
— Joe Frazier

Problems are a part of life. Expect them. Welcome them. If we did not have them, we would not be alive. Romeo, my employee and head boxing trainer at my gym, always jokes about how I wake up bobbing and weaving, and I do, but first I meditate, juice celery, and honor my self-care.

Boxers are nonstop bobbing and weaving and slipping and moving. Otherwise they get knocked out. They are avoiding getting hit and then are moving to strategically create angles, and openings so they can hit their opponents instead of getting hit themselves. They bob and weave, then hit or stick and move to hit, and avoid getting hit.

Not everything that comes at you needs you to solve it. Know the difference. Slip and move, and do not get knocked out. Slip what is coming at you and make the necessary moves to get back on top and winning. You either run the day, or the day runs you. Do not get hit head-on or smacked in the face; rather, anticipate, see it coming, and then

Bob and weave, stick and move.

#7
OWN YOUR POWER

Promoters need you. You don't need them, the boxer has
the leverage, and a lot of boxers don't know that.
— Ryan Garcia

Know your power and own it. Annihilate and destroy any stories that disempower you or limit you.

Empowering emotions sound like the following:

- "I so got this."
- "I'm smart."
- "I'll figure it out; I always do."
- "I'm a beast."
- "I will win."
- "I am so inspired about my future."

Disempowering emotions sound like these:

- "I wanna die."
- "This is such a mess."
- "Freedom is over."
- "I hate it here."
- "My life is over."
- "Everyone is so annoying."
- "I am so irritated."

You need an emotion stronger than the disempowering emotions to get rid of them and regain your own power. The empowering emotions need to dominate the disempowering ones. Through self-talk, self-discipline, and movement, you must intervene with *yourself* and empower *yourself.* Take charge and *be the boss of you!* Generate and motivate yourself to own your own power, and when you feel powerless, know how to take back your power.

Ask yourself, "What are my top feel-good emotions that, if I put myself in that state of being, would cause those disempowering emotions to disappear?" For me they are gratitude, joy, surrender, decisiveness, powerful, whole, and unlimited.

Your emotional state affects everything. When you get in a certain state, your story changes accordingly. So the secret is to first change your state, and then you can change your story. Practice feeling elevated emotions with clear intentions. *Feeling is everything.*

The fastest way to change your state is to *move your body* and get into a strong and powerful state. Stand up straight, the posture of strength and power, and get moving so you can feel better. Movement is medicine.

Use affirmations and incantations to affirm and remind yourself of your own power. Incantations are series of words said as a magical spell. They involve your entire being, not just saying the words. Practice them daily, hundreds of times over and over again. Say them with passion and move your body to match. Explode that part of yourself. Build that muscle so that part of you shows up, rather than the disempowering part of you.

Ask yourself, "Why do I *really* want what I say I want?" You need to be emotionally fit and then own your power. Like in the dating world, I teach girls and young women self-respect and honor and to preserve themselves for only the super special in due time. If more girls and women would realize that they have the leverage when they own their own power, the dating scene would dramatically change. We get in life what we accept and tolerate. If we did not accept things or tolerate them, they would not keep showing up in our realities.

Know your power, and then *own your power.*

Boxers are extremely powerful, and they never give their power away; otherwise, they would lose for sure. Boxers know their power, generate power, and feel powerful because they are. We sell shirts that say "Boxers Hit It Harder" because they do.

I always loved a quote by Marianne Williamson in *A Return to Love:*

> Our deepest fear is not that we are inadequate. Our
> deepest fear is that we are powerful beyond measure. It
> is our light, not our darkness, that most frightens us.
> We ask ourselves, "Who am I to be brilliant, gorgeous,
> talented, fabulous?" Actually, who are you not to be?
> You are a child of God. You playing small does not serve
> the world. There is nothing enlightened about shrinking
> so that other people won't feel insecure around you. We
> are all meant to shine, as children do. We were born to

make manifest the glory of God that is within us. It's not just in some of us; it's in everyone. And as we let our own light shine, we unconsciously give other people permission to do the same. As we are liberated from our own fear, our presence automatically liberates others.

Know that you are powerful beyond measure and *own your power.*

#8
THE FOUNDATION AND
BASICS ARE EVERYTHING

People have just said about me so far that I'm just a big puncher, but I showed that I can command a fight behind my jab, which is the foundation of all good boxing.
— Daniel Dubois

The parts of the whole are as important as the whole itself. It is like phonics versus whole language for early childhood development in language and communication. Both are important. You would not want one without the other. The foundation, framework, breakdown of the parts, and basics are super important. They are the roots, where it all originates. To understand things best, you want to know what created them in the first place and how it was done. Then you will have a much better picture and understanding of the whole.

In boxing, styles make fights, which means rules go out the window in some fashion as boxers put their own flair on the fight, yet their style is still balanced and makes sense for it to work. Many variables are involved. Boxing is called *sweet science* as it takes logic and science to create an environment where it is all possible. The sweet science of boxing requires boxers to be tough, tactical, and fierce, and they also must be able to anticipate their opponents' next moves. It is very important to constantly practice the basics and work at getting better at them, as they create what comes from them and what comes after them. The basics and foundation need to be on point for anything that follows them to work. Boxers create moments and movements, and every punch sets up the next, just like in life. Everything we do has an effect on everything else that follows, and it all stems from how we began.

The foundation and basics are everything.

#9
COMMITMENT TO EXCELLENCE

I am gonna show you how great I am.
— Muhammad Ali

Don't you understand anything about commitment, about being a pro, about sticking with what you say you wanna be? You don't just say it when you feel good. You don't just say it when you're not tired. You don't do it just when it's not sunny. You do it everyday of your life. You do it when it hurts to do it, when it's the last thing in the world you wanna do, when there are a million reasons not to do it. You do it because you're a professional.
— Teddy Atlas

Do only what aligns with what you are committed to and your goals. You must commit to accomplish anything, and once you commit fully, there is no way you will not complete all you set out to do. Do not allow quitting to be an option. Do not let opportunities disappear. Do something immediately that commits you to follow through in the desirable direction. Commitment stays when emotions and feelings back out. When you are committed, you do what you set out to do regardless of whether you feel like it in the moment or not.

Commitment is the way. Excellence is the way. Commitment shows up in your life in what you do.

How you spend your time is what you are committed to doing. People fear commitment, as then they have to deliver. They say, "I'll try." Well, *try* to sit down. You either do or do not.

A sign in my boxing gym says, "There's no try, there's either do or don't." So often people go to a gym and say, "I'll try to come." I let them know that if they *try*, it is not going to happen. It needs to be scheduled and then completed.

When I was a kid and I got a 99 on a paper, my mom would say, "Why not 100?" And she was right. It is not about disempowering and feeling not good enough; it is that we can always be better. What is missing, the presence of which would make all the difference, is what it takes to get the 100.

Just do it, and oftentimes, *just do it now*.

Excuses are conditioned ways of being. They prevent you from excellence. Do not have them or use them for anything you said you would do; rather, commit to being excellent. If you are going to do something and spend time on it, do it excellently. Choose, rather than excuse, to do it. Create that habit instead.

It's funny—I always want to put together bloopers of people coming into my gym to inquire about joining. They always express all they want and how they want to lose weight and get fit, and then they kill off any possibility of obtaining all they want with their excuses.

The funniest excuse is "I don't commit." I tell them, "Yes, you do. You wipe your butt always and brush your teeth. You are committed to that! You know you do not want poop in your underwear, so you're committed to wiping your butt. You commit. You brush your teeth every day. You commit." I also tell them they are committed to saying they don't commit. I tell them, "Committing is a great thing. It is how you get to where you want, and you do not get desirable results without being committed to getting them."

Boxers commit fully. They must in order to win and become champions. Want to commit. Love to commit. Know it is what gets you to where you want to be. Use your words to create your world.

Be excellent.

Strive for excellence.

Commit to excellence.

Always do the right thing.

People notice.

Let excellence be your brand.

When you are excellent, you become unforgettable, and that is what we all want. *Commit to being excellent.* Do the right things, even when nobody knows. It will always bring the right things to you. Newton's third law of motion, "for every action there is an equal and opposite reaction," applies to all our lives. Do your best always, and the best will come back to you. Grow yourself into the best of yourself.

I want to love my life so that when I leave this world my aura is at its brightest. Be addicted to getting great. Wake up obsessed.

Get hooked on the process. Be so excited for what is next to come.

Here are some excuses followed by affirmations and reframing to get rid of the excuse.

- "I am too busy." What you are busy with is a result of all your choices. Are you too busy to be happy? Say instead, affirm, "I intend to take time for myself."
- "It will be difficult." Say instead, affirm, "I have the ability to accomplish anything with grace and ease" or "So what if it's difficult? I am great under pressure and I so got this."
- "It's going to be risky." Say instead, affirm, "Being myself involves no risk."

- "It will take a long time." Say instead, affirm, "The journey of a thousand miles begins with one step" or "I got this—slow and steady wins the race."
- "The rules will not let me." Say instead, affirm, "I live my life according to divine rules."

We get what we deserve and seek, not what we need.

Deserve it; do not need it. Work for it; do not hope or wish for it. Hope blows. Hope is for beggars. Instead of hoping, commit to excellence and make things happen.

Put your commitments before your comfort. Sometimes you do not want to put forth the effort, and you would rather surf social media, watch a movie, or take a nap. Yet if you have set a time to work on something, do not put it off until you feel like doing it. Just do it by when you originally said you would do it. When you put things off, as you know from experience, *later* often becomes *never*.

Wake up early. Give yourself plenty of time in the morning for yourself and to not have to rush. Every morning, reflect on what is going on with you personally in your journal, and prepare for your day with meditation. Create a sanctuary for yourself. My home is always filled with fresh flowers, candles, and lovely scents of aromatherapy. Be crystal clear on your big vision, and divide everything you do into small, manageable actions. When you work, do it in chunks of uninterrupted, distraction-free time blocks. Handle or shut off anything that will distract you. Make no excuses. Excuses are simply fear of failure or fear of success hiding out underneath.

Work in teams. Everything I do is done in collaboration. It may look like I am a one-woman show, but behind the scenes are many people on whom I call for assistance, to partner with, and to cocreate. Teamwork makes the dream work. Ask for support, lots of it, from your friends, your family, and your partner. Speak up when you need help, and do not do everything yourself. Be resourceful. It's never a matter of resources, it's a matter of resourcefulness.

Demand of yourself excellent results and performance. If you want an extraordinary life and results, you need to be extraordinary and do extraordinary things. Perform year after year after year. Ask it of yourself. I can inspire you and share with you, *but* you must demand it of yourself and then act accordingly. Demand all you want. Demand of yourself. Success is an inside job. People want the convenience of success without the inconvenience of hard work. Do not be one of those people.

Decide. Commit. Act. Succeed. Repeat.

Turn your *should*s into *must*s. Pursue great ideas and opportunities, as they are not going to find you. Sweat the small stuff, meaning the details. Pay attention to everything. The devil's work is in the details.

Focus on everything. Everything matters. Be outstanding. Accept nothing less. We get what we tolerate. Demand the greatest of yourself. *Commit to excellence.*

#10
KNOW YOURSELF

The whole key is to be honest with yourself, find the weak spots, work on it, get it done.
— Wladimir Klitschko

My wealth is in my knowledge of self, love, and spirituality.
— Muhammad Ali

You are only on this planet to be you. Everything else is an imitation. The best way to truly know yourself is to sit in silence. Meditate. *Meditate* means to become familiar with, and then you can sustain the elevated emotions and stay in action. Learn and know what you like and what you do not like, and then experiences bring you wisdom and knowledge of yourself. Know how you like to be treated, what you do that works, what you do that does not work, and so on. You are limitless and endless and possess everything you need inside yourself. Dive in deep, become your own best friend, and get to know yourself. We are the universe's parts that get to know themselves better. Listen. The quieter you become, the more you can hear.

Know yourself.

#11
BE STRATEGIC

In boxing you create a strategy to beat each
new opponent; it's just like chess.
— Lennox Lewis

Strategy is the way you will execute something, and it makes sense. I love to always create a win-win situation. In communicating, I am strategic in my word choice so that it serves me and honors me first and then also serves and honors the other person and what it is I am wanting to accomplish in the interaction. I say be strategic in all endeavors. It involves prethinking. It is visualizing. It is weighing out options and studying what is yet to come for a most optimal outcome. It is coming up with a way and opportunities to accomplish what you want. You do not want to go into anything ill prepared. It is all about the way—the way you think about it. Change your thoughts methodically, and that changes everything. It is all about the strategy. Come up with the pictures and decisions you want to come to fruition prior to the event.

In boxing, the jab is the most important punch as it is the one that sets up everything that comes after it. The jab allows boxers to measure the distance and close the distance, and it leads them into and out of the line of fire. In boxing and in life, styles make fights; therefore, a different strategy is needed for each opponent and fight. Boxers do not go into each fight the same way. They study their opponents and come up with a specific strategy to win against that specific fighter. But God laughs when we make plans, so all the other rules come into play as well, such as always be ready and prepare for the unexpected. Yet you still must always have a strategy to create leverage and win. Be like a boxer in life and

Be strategic.

#12
DIG DEEP

*You know that the power comes from within: when
you are tired, or you want to give up.
Dig deep. Dig deep for whatever reason—in boxing, in sport, in life.*
— Joseph Parker

Give it your all. You never want regrets, so do not do anything that will make you regretful. When you think you have nothing left, dig down deep inside and give it more. Bob Marley said, "You never know how strong you are until being strong is your only choice." Make being strong your only choice. No excuses. When you have them, recognize them as excuses and know that you got this. You just have to dig deep and give it all you got. Why would you not?

Boxers always need to dig deep. They perform under extreme pressure and carry on, pushing past their limits. Their job is triumphing while keeping their eyes open in a situation that is like a car crash. Boxers never give up; they just keep pushing forward and dig deep inside of themselves to deliver. Know that you have whatever it takes inside you to achieve all you want. You just need to

Dig deep.

#13
FIGHT, THINK, LEARN, AND BE SMART

I'm on the record for five losses or something like that, but the one guy who really whipped me was Muhammad Ali. And it taught me one big lesson. That no matter how big and strong you are, you're going to have to use your mind. You must think things out.
— George Foreman

You have good days, you have bad days.
But the main thing is to grow mentally.
— Floyd Mayweather Jr.

Everybody thinks this is a tough man's sport. This is not a tough man's sport. This is a thinking man's sport. A tough man is gonna get hurt real bad in this sport.
— Mike Tyson

Think smart. The only way to think smart is to learn and accumulate knowledge and wisdom. We all know the saying, "Common sense isn't very common." Do not be lazy. I live by Jim Rohn's advice: "Work harder on yourself than you do on your job and life becomes easier." To be smart, you need to learn, put it into practice, and use it to think smart. Learn from others who have already been successful, as success leaves clues. Do not keep repeating the same mistakes. Learn from them. Grow from them. Turn your woes into wisdom. Wisdom is your knowledge gained from past experiences without an emotional charge. We've all heard that making the same (wrong) choice over and over again and expecting a different result is the definition of insanity. Learn. Do better. Know better. Be wise. When I took courses for my NLP Master Practitioner License from the creator himself, Richard Bandler, he said, "In short, NLP means stop doing stupid shit and do/think something smarter."

If you change the way you think, you change the way you feel, and therefore you can stop or start anything. Think on purpose. Think purposely. Use your brain. Challenge it. Study happy, successful people, not unhappy, successful people. Model what you do want, not what you do not want. Think better. Change what you are thinking and how you are thinking, and everything changes. Slow down enough to notice your thoughts. Think of what you do want, not what you do not want. Go after what you do want and learn as much as you can, from as many people you can, whenever you can. There are more neurons in your brain than stars in the sky. Your brain works faster than you think. Thinking is a choice.

Boxers need to fight smart, think smart, and be smart in their approaches and strategies. Boxing is for sure a mental sport. Boxers must continuously mentally prepare for their specific opponents and fights. Boxers study, practice, perform, and reflect on what they can do differently in the future. Do that in your life.

Fight, think, learn, and be smart.

#14
DON'T BE A FOLLOWER

Don't follow the crowd; let them follow you.
— George Foreman

I never was a person that wanted that life. I'm a leader not a follower. I don't care what they say, or what they're doing or what they're wearing. Go ahead, cos come Judgment Day, all of that won't matter. How many people did you help? How many people did you talk to? How many people did you try to encourage? How many people did you bring to God? That's what's gon' matter.
— Roy Jones Jr.

I always say it is no coincidence that the concept of having followers on social media creates a world of followers. We need a social media platform of leaders supporting leaders, not followers. Everyone can be a leader, and we need them to be. Lead by example. Be the change. I had a bumper sticker on my car when I was a teenager that said, "If the people lead, the leaders will follow." It's similar to the concept of emergence, where parts of a system do together what they would not do alone. Properties or behaviors emerge only when the parts interact in a wider whole. They are all needed and are all leading. You are the creator of your life. Be fully self-expressed for who you are and your expression in the world. The difference between humans and animals is animals would never allow the dumbest of the herd to lead them. Do not do or be what others do or feel you should be. It is your life and your responsibility, 100 percent.

Boxers for sure are not followers. They have teams behind them but are each really a one-person show. They lead and are confident enough to follow their dreams regardless of what anyone else thinks or says. In life, be authentically you, be fully self-expressed, be a leader, and

Don't be a follower.

#15
NEVER USE THE SAME TIMING, RHYTHM, OR TEMPO

Rhythm is everything in boxing. Every move you make starts with your heart, and that's in rhythm or you're in trouble.
— Sugar Ray Robinson

My philosophy and motto I live by and share, as evidenced by a tattoo I have, is, "The moments between the notes create the music." It is what's between the notes that *create* the dance or music; and in sports, it is the moments and spaces between the movements that create the actual dance or flow.

A boxer's workout and life *never* use the same timing, rhythm, or tempo. *Train for that!* Boxers cannot be timed if they want to win, so they always have to be sneaky and calculated and mix things up. Boxers mix it all up and outwit their opponents with variety in rhythm, timing, and tempo. Music is made up as much of silence as it is out of sound. Honor the space; it is needed. Create space; it is needed.

Never use the same timing, rhythm, or tempo.

#16
TRAIN TO WIN

Champions aren't made in gyms. Champions are made from something they have deep inside them—a desire, a dream, a vision.
— Muhammad Ali

The fight is won or lost far away from witnesses—behind the lines, in the gym, and out there on the road, long before I dance under those lights.
— Muhammad Ali

Train to win. Do whatever it takes to prepare your mind, body, and spirit to win at whatever it is you are setting yourself up to accomplish. Know what you want out of the situation and go after it obsessively. Study, learn, practice, and train when nobody else is. Feel your win. See your win. Imagine your win. Taste your win. Savor it and chase whom you need to become to accomplish the win.

Nobody trains to lose. Boxers focus on winning, and they train to win. Everybody loves the feeling of winning, but not everybody is willing to compete for it. Be someone who will. When Mike Tyson was answering members' questions at my gym, he said, "You have to be a champion before you're a champion, and you have to have a champion lifestyle." People do not just stumble upon being a champion; they live, act, behave, and practice like a champion to become recognized as one. They live as champions, and they

Train to win.

#17
BE INTENTIONAL

You have to know you can win. You have to think
you can win. You have to feel you can win.
— Sugar Ray Leonard

In every moment, know what you are going after, and go after it with laser focus and vision. Prethink. Do what you do with purpose, on purpose, intentionally. Do not just go through the motions of things. Be intentional with every thought and move you make. Intention is not something to do; it is something to connect to and align with to create desired outcomes. Combine a clear intention with an elevated emotion, and *practice feeling amazing*. The longer you can stay in the feeling, the more magic and synchronicities will show up in your life. The goal is to create stronger and more intense internal events that are positive to overpower the negative ones. Your feelings are what attract your events back to you. It's the law of attraction. Do not send mixed messages into the universe. *Be clear. Live in the feelings of gratitude, joy, and inspiration, and just feel good*! Become self-aware. Be deliberate, calculated, planned, willful, and willing; *be intentional*.

When we live with intent, we own our actions instead of habitually performing them. Everything we do benefits from the presence of intent, which has the power to transform seemingly mundane tasks into profound experiences. We only have to try it to find out. We must acknowledge what we are doing while we are doing it. As we do, we come alive to our bodies and the world. We need to realize and notice how often we act without intention and how this disengages us from reality. Applying the energy of intent to even one task a day has the power to transform our lives. Then imagine applying that energy of intent to all we do in our days. *Wowsie*!

Boxers are super intentional. They know exactly what they are going to do beforehand, and they do it with intent. Boxers are deliberate; they know what combinations they will throw before their opponents even attack and throw theirs. Boxers are very calculated, and they are clear upfront about what they are about to achieve. It is important, in order for a boxer to win, to

Be intentional.

#18
SEE EVERYTHING

The hand can't hit what the eye can't see.
— Muhammad Ali

The punch that knocks a man out is the punch that he didn't see.
— Cus D'Amato

Always be focused and pay close attention. Become aware. Boxers see everything. Their vision is superperipheral. When they are fighting, they cannot blink or lose focus because they will get knocked out. Imagine that, for a boxer in a fight, it is like keeping your eyes open in a car crash for extended periods of time. You need convergent focus and divergent focus. You need to see a closeup and an expanded, even disassociated, view all at the same time. See it all. Practice. Do not blink. Notice what is all around you and right in front of your face. Boxers get knocked out only by the punches they do not see, just like in life. Do not get blindsided. Keep your eyes open, be aware, and

See everything.

#19
PRACTICE IS KEY, AND YOU CAN
NEVER PRACTICE ENOUGH

There are always improvements to make; no boxer
in the world does everything right.
— Luke Campbell

Mastery comes from repetition. When you are rewarded in public, you are actually being rewarded for what you practiced in private. Champions are made when no one is watching. Repetition is the mother of all skill. It is the mother of mastery. Practice, practice, practice. You can never practice enough. We have a saying in fighting that when you are not training, someone else is training to kick your ass. Boxers are always training, and they never stop. It is their lifestyle, and it is necessary to win. No days off. No slacking—not if you want to win and be a champion. You need consistency in practicing and working on your craft. You are whom you practice to be. Hard work pays off—you have for sure heard that before, and it does. There is always more to get to and achieve and become. Practice making better choices and making better pictures and visuals in your head. Practice anything and everything you want to become better at and excel at, down to your breathing. Practice that consciously too. Know that

Practice is key, and you can never practice enough.

#20
BE RESILIENT

A setback only paves the way for a comeback.
— Evander Holyfield

*I got knocked down. Anybody could be knocked down,
anybody can be knocked out, but it's not what
happened, but what happens next.*
— Bernard Hopkins

If you never know failure, you will never know success.
— Sugar Ray Leonard

We all have struggles in life, but we need to continue to fight. Like Rocky Balboa said, "It ain't about how hard you can hit. It's about how hard you can get hit and keep moving forward." Like I say, the moments between the notes create the music, and you do not want to flatline; you want to keep it moving. You need to take a moment, reflect, get back in the game, and keep creating. You cannot allow yourself to stay stuck, and you need to do whatever it takes to get unstuck. Life is not about what happens; it is about how we react to what happens. Our circumstances do not make us who we are; they reveal who we are. So take the hit and come back stronger.

Boxers are very resilient. Imagine how many get knocked out and come back to win championship belts. The loss just makes them hungry to come back and win. It is always about the comeback and never about the setback, especially when the comeback is so amazing. Be amazing.

Be resilient.

#21
FACE YOUR FEARS
HEAD~ON

Fear is like fire; it can be helpful if you know
how to use it. If not you'll get burned.
— Mike Tyson

The hero and the coward both feel the same thing. But the hero uses
his fear, projects it onto his opponent, while the coward runs. It's
the same thing, fear, but it's what you do with it that matters.
— Cus D'Amato

Fear is imagination undirected. Faith is imagination directed. So face your fears and have faith. Give up your stories of limitation. Fear stops you from achieving what you want. As humans, our two primary fears are, "I'm not enough," and, "If I am not enough, I won't be loved."

You cannot skip over fear. You need to face it, deal with it, and move on to the next challenge, as life is a continual presentation of challenges. Expect them and deal with them head-on. No matter how bad it is, know you will make it through and it will all be fine. Dance with your fear, align with it, and go with it. The stories we use to protect us often imprison us. *Feel* the fear, yet move forward and take action anyway. When the fear of failure is real, ask yourself, "What is the worst that could happen if I fail?" Then ask yourself, "Can I handle that?" The answer is always yes. *Of course, you can.*

Boxers face their fears head-on every time they step in the ring. Of course they have fear, but they don't let it stop them. Mike Tyson told me that when his opponents would try to use fear as a fighting tactic to win, it would only work against them as it just made him even more vicious and unstoppable. Boxers use fear, face their fears, and keep moving forward and attacking what is in front of them. Conquering fear brings confidence and growth. The only fears we were born with are fear of loud sounds and fear of falling; all others are fears we make up and are not real. Fear stands for *false evidence appearing real*. Know this. Do not make things heavy and significant. Choose to take risks. Do not wait for proof. Do not hit the regret stage and then review the wish you would have had if you have taken risks. Ask yourself how many of your greatest fears ever really happened. Really, how many?

Face your fears head-on.

#22
BELIEVE IT,
THEN YOU WILL SEE IT

It's the repetition of affirmations that leads to belief. And once that belief becomes a deep conviction, things begin to happen.
— Muhammad Ali

I am the greatest, I said that even before I knew I was.
— Muhammad Ali

Our thoughts carry frequency and information. Choose your thoughts the way you want them to manifest. Believe them and have gratitude for them, and you will see them. We create our worlds and the world around us with our beliefs and perceptions.

You need to first believe it, and then you can see it manifest for yourself and your life. You must think, know, and feel that you can have whatever you want for yourself and your life, with no limitations. That is how boxers live. They believe they will be champions from the beginning, and then they do whatever it takes to become champions. They believe it, see it, imagine it, and taste it way before it comes to fruition. It is their strong belief that motivates them and pushes them through the tough times and setbacks.

We often create by default, by not consciously creating. So meditate and create consciously so you can be the magician of your own life.

Believe it, then you will see it.

#23
ADJUST AND RESPOND
BEST UNDER PRESSURE

Tough times don't last, tough people do.
— Floyd Mayweather Jr.

We are all controlled by our states. The best skill set is to be able to quickly change your state to a conducive, more desirable state. When under pressure, you do not want to get stuck or stopped. You want to be able to respond quickly and most efficiently, rather than folding under pressure. Notice when you get stumped and you do not respond best under pressure. What happens? What words do you say to yourself? Notice and listen. Create language that empowers you and has you respond assertively and directly, without wavering on nerves and fears. Practice getting great at that.

Boxers are always being pressured, and they are always having to adjust and respond super quickly and effectively to avoid getting knocked out. They train for this; they practice and prepare for this over and over again. Do this in your life. Pressure is what creates diamonds. Withstand and excel under pressure, and great things will come. Practice these scenarios and become great in your ability to

Adjust and respond best under pressure.

#24
NO ONE IS COMING
TO SAVE YOU

Once the bell rings you're on your own.
It's just you and the other guy.
— Joe Louis

You got this! I always say, "We are born alone, we die alone, and we are never alone." There is a huge difference between being alone and being lonely. Being alone is a beautiful thing. You have yourself to count on, and *you rock!* Know that it is your life and only yours. Take responsibility and be actively, intentionally in the driver's seat. No one is coming to save you. Know this and allow it to empower you to see that everything you need is already inside of you.

A boxer enters a ring with just an opponent—and a referee, of course. Yet it is the two fighters alone, and they are clear that they must fight to the finish. Boxers know that they are risking their lives every time they step into that ring, and they know it is up to them, and them alone, to win. Know that you have all that it takes to accomplish and get through all you want and that comes your way. It is all up to you, and

No one is coming to save you.

#25
SELF-CONTROL IS REQUIRED
—STAY CALM

Boxing definitely has a part to play in taking
away unwanted aggression.
— Joe Calzaghe

Boxers need to constantly remain calm when they get hit. They need to keep their composure always, even in the midst of the fire. I feel that is one of the hardest things in boxing. It takes years of experience and practice. Imagine the power of staying calm and under control in the midst of a fight. It is possible, as boxers do it in all their fights, and we all want to be able to do that in life. The ego says, "once everything falls into place, I will feel peace," and the spirit says, "find your peace and then everything will fall into place." It is *causing an effect not cause and effect*. Notice what triggers you. Work on not getting activated. Like Eleanor Roosevelt said, "No one can make you feel inferior without your consent." Know that when we lose composure and self-control, we give our power away, and we give the other party permission to control our state of being. Self-control is required. You cannot win and be successful without it. People who do not take control of their lives live out of control. How other people see you is important; it is your image. Have the image of someone who is in control, in charge, and disciplined. People want to be around others in control. Our tagline for the Jolie's Kids charity is "We teach kids to fight, so they don't." They practice self-control. As Lao Tzu said, "The best fighters are never angry."

Self-control is required. Stay calm.

#26
NOTHING WORKS
WITHOUT INTEGRITY

It's not bragging if you can back it up.
— Muhammad Ali

Integrity is honoring your word. It is doing what you said you would do by when you would do it by and keeping an empowering context. Everything lives in communication, and nothing exists without it. We create our world with our words whether we know it or not. You are your word, or you're not. You have integrity, or you do not. Your life works, or it does not. In the areas where it does not work, integrity is missing. Look inside to see which areas of your life are not working, and then determine where you are not being your word. Then decide if you really want that area to work. If so, you need to take action and do only what you say you will do; otherwise, don't say it. When you are in communication, you bring into existence the story of the words you say. All integrity does is create workability. Honor yourself and honor your words. Choose them wisely. They are yours to choose, and they are creating your life.

You do not do things because you are motivated, as often times you will not be at all and you have to do them anyway. You do it because you said you would and because you want the results and desired outcomes. You need to have a "must do it" not a "should do it" mindset to guarantee it gets done. People say, "I don't commit" or "I don't stick to things." If that is the case, their lives do not work in all those areas.

Be aware of your words, both in your head and what comes out of your mouth. Words have meaning, and they all carry a vibration. Which vibrations do you want to live into, exist in, and put into existence? Say them in the mirror. Use the positive ones in your life and in your daily thoughts, pictures, and speaking.

Boxers possess integrity. They need to honor their words, their training regimens, and all they set out to do if they want to win and become champions. Integrity is your character. Be a person of high values, principles, and honesty. Be a person who earns respect. Have character to do the right thing. People will see you as honest, fair, willing to be helpful, and willing to always walk the center line. With integrity, you will last longer and be stronger. You will have return customers and consistently increasing results. People need to be able to count on you. Build and develop your own character.

Have integrity.
Honor yourself.
Honor your words.
Be your word.
You're the boss of you.
Govern yourself accordingly.
Nothing works without integrity.

JOLIE

(J) G

GLASSMAN

#27
LIFE IS NOT FAIR:
PLAY FULL OUT ANYWAY

Hating people because of their color is wrong. And it doesn't matter which color does the hating. It's just plain wrong.
— Muhammad Ali

Life is not fair. No one said it would be. That does not mean you should be lazy or pull out of the game. Do your best regardless. Play full out regardless. Hard work pays off. People will notice. Even if you have setbacks due to unfairness, keep pushing forward and know you will prevail. Good wins. God wins. Follow the light. Be the light. In sports we say, "Go hard, or go home." You do not want to be a bad sport or a sore loser. Just give it your all and do your best, and that is all anyone can ask of you. Do not let the behaviors of others affect your decisions and output of work. Stay in your lane, and know that even though life is not fair, you are going to play full out no matter what.

Boxers are confronted with lots of unfairness as it is a sport in which the winner is decided by judges. Sometimes there are bad decisions, but the boxer needs to just keep fighting and come back stronger. Boxers often do not get the chance when they deserve it, and they do not get the win even if they deserved it. Often boxers feel they need to knock out their opponents if they want to prevail, especially if they know their opponents are favored. Boxers do not let that stop them; they fight anyway. They are fighters. Turn your woes into a source of wisdom.

Life is not fair. Play full out anyway.

#28
BE COACHABLE

I consider myself a student of boxing, a philosopher so to speak, and my philosophy is to keep learning.
— Manny Paquiao

Boxers have trainers on whom they rely to advise them and help perfect their craft. They also have their coaches in their corners when they are fighting to guide them and tell them what they can do to win. Coaches can see what boxers do not. They motivate the fighters to keep pushing through, to do certain combinations, and to avoid certain punches from their opponents. Boxing coaches assist in keeping their boxers on track and committed to their training regimen. Boxers must be coachable as no trainer wants to work with one who is not.

Every coach needs a coach. You want to be coachable rather than stubborn. You can always learn from everyone and everything, yet if you are not coachable, you resist the learning. You want to listen and learn as much as possible, as it is up to you to keep or reject what it is you are hearing and learning. You decide, but at least be coachable enough to decipher. No one wants to train or coach a student who is not coachable, nor does someone want to hire someone who is not coachable. Be able to take feedback. Nothing added, nothing taken away—just listen and receive.

Be coachable.

#29
TOUCH GLOVES,
HONOR, RESPECT

*The thing about boxers is there's respect there. You beat
me, and I may not like it, but you know what, deep down
inside, I respect you. And that's the code of honor.*
— Sugar Ray Leonard

Honor yourself and honor others. Treat yourself and others like you all matter because you do. You matter because you are here. Without respect and honor for other people, true leadership becomes ineffective and probably impossible. Boxers always touch gloves prior to fighting to show respect to each other and basically say, "Good luck." Boxing is an honorable sport. It is a gentleman's sport. It is where boys were turned into men in the army.

Honor is taking pride, valuing, and respecting. Honor yourself first and then honor the world. *Namaste!* Honor the light within yourself that also honors the light within others, as you share the same light. Just like on an airplane, in case of an emergency, you are instructed to first cover your own mouth and nose with the oxygen mask and then help your children and others. *You first!* Treat yourself the way you want to be treated by others. As the saying goes, "If mama ain't happy, no one is happy." *Create a win-win outcome.* Create it in such a way that it honors who you are and your expression in the world. Serve the world around you, and then receive joy in return. *Service* equals *joy* and, for me, also a life of fulfillment.

You cannot give what you do not have. Fill your cup first. The people who want the best for you want you to be your best. So surround yourself with people who will fill your cup. Then know that once your cup is filled, you then have plenty to give. Take an inventory of what you do have, and then give it away and serve. It will all come back tenfold.

Primarily rely on yourself so that you can never complain and never have to explain. Take responsibility and honor *yourself.* Always come from a loving space. See yourself as love and having only that to give away. Assume everyone has the best intentions. Know you are a piece of the divine, part of the unlimited source, but it becomes limited by your thoughts and beliefs. We are spiritual beings having a temporary human experience. Do not do bad things; only do good things. Live with honor. Be like a boxer,

Touch gloves, honor, and respect.

#30
HIT AND DON'T GET HIT

The first thing I learned in boxing is to not get hit. That's the art of boxing. Execute your opponent without getting hit.
— Wladimir Klitchko

You've got to be smart, and not get hit, and when you're able to do this, you're a fighter.
— Cus D'Amato

76

This is the main premise in boxing, to hit and not get hit. Boxers want to be able to hit their opponents and connect and then protect themselves in such a way that they cannot get hit back. Every time boxers hit and throw punches, they leave themselves open to get hit back. Boxers need to be smart and move so that they do not get hit, as that is the name of the game of boxing.

In life, you want to be able to attack the task at hand without getting attacked in return. Be like a boxer—

Hit and don't get hit.

#31
ALWAYS MOTIVATE YOURSELF

In order to be at the top and maintain your focus
you have to have something that motivates you.
— Marvelous Marvin Hagler

Fake it until you make it. Do what you need to do and what you said you would do, whether you want to or not. Find ways to motivate yourself. I love music, so music always motivates me. I always play a specific genre of music to motivate me to get into whatever mood I need for stretching, working out, getting ready for work, or working. If you have to do something and you plan to do it, you might as well do it, get it done as quickly as possible, and self-motivate. Have phrases and motivating commands to say to yourself to get motivated and get into action as quickly as possible. Chase the desire to transform so that the motivation comes to you. Be inspired by your future that is to come. Whenever I need to do something that I do not want to do, I say, "I don't want to do it. Ugh, I have to do this. *I'm doing it now.*" Get out of the funk before it takes over and you become too lazy.

Boxers do not rely on motivation even though they are motivated as they have passion and desire to become champions. That is the carrot in front that motivates them. They are always chasing after something, and they have lofty goals; therefore, they are motivated to achieve them. They do not train only when they are motivated; they just train always, regardless of whether motivation is present. They need to, or they will not win.

Motivation comes after you do what you had said you wanted to do. Motivation is never there when you need it. Make yourself move, and get moving, as movement is access to motivation. When you feel like quitting think of why you started. Have passion. When you love what you do and are passionate about it, you are motivated. Empower yourself. Do not wait for others to praise you. Tell yourself everyday, "I am enough, and I got this."

Always motivate yourself.

#32
HAVE PASSION—
LOVE WHAT YOU DO

*I've had boxing gloves on since before I could
walk, and been in gyms all of my life.*
— Floyd Mayweather Jr.

*I'm always having fun in training and in boxing.
I think it's because boxing is my passion.*
— Manny Paquiao

Boxers are extremely passionate, and they love what they do as it is a full-time job and it is their life. Boxers box their entire lives—from a very young age until they retire. They desire to become champions so much that they obsess over it. They love it and have a hard time retiring from it. Many of them stay in the game too long due to their passion, their love for the sport, and all the excitement and fame. Boxers love the crowds, the bright lights, the fans, and the attention.

My life is fueled by my being, my being fuels the doing, and I come from compassion and understanding. Without love and passion, what do we have? Passion unexpressed diminishes. Desire something badly and then obsess about it like boxers do. The way you move determines the way you feel. Everything is about your emotional state. Performance is directly related to your state. You live in the world you create. There is always the "what happened" and then the "what you made what happened mean." Those are two different worlds. Make the world you live in a passionate one. You are making it up anyhow, so you might as well make it awesome. Your choice. When I was in my Landmark Education studies, we used to say, "Have a good day, or not."

You need to be immersed in your craft and the mastering of it, so having passion and loving it is necessary. Have hunger. Be hungry. Have enthusiasm and be passionate about your endeavors. Know you will get the job done. Know you will affect people. Enjoying and loving what you do makes what you do feel all like play and nothing like work. If you are committing to this fully, then you do not want to feel like you are always and only working. You want to feel like all you do is for the love of the game, and then everything that comes with it is a bonus.

Have passion. Love what you do.

#33
MINDSET IS EVERYTHING

When a man says I cannot, he has made a suggestion to himself. He has weakened his power of accomplishing that which otherwise would have been accomplished.
— Muhammad Ali

Anything is possible with the right mindset.
— Tyson Fury

Boxers must believe in themselves and have a strong, positive mindset to win; without it, they would lose. They believe they will be champions way before they are. Boxers' mindsets are extremely strong. In a way, they fight wars for a living. They think first and then act accordingly. Every day they need to push hard and monitor their mindsets, not allowing them to falter. In their minds, they see exactly how they will beat each opponent. Boxers are always mentally visualizing their wins.

What you think and believe determine the quality of your life and your personality. Whether you think you can or cannot, you are right. Nothing is impossible with the right approach and mindset. If you are going to succeed, you need to see things better than they are. First see them as they are, and then have the vision to see them as better than they are, not worse. Make things the way you want them. Our minds are so powerful, and we are creating things with our mindsets, beliefs, and perceptions. Have a positive, forward-moving, triumphant mindset, and then make all things that you want possible. Do things in your mind first and then make your body follow. We are the creators of our lives, not just the managers of our circumstances. Create with a mindset that is happy, powerful, abundant, grateful, clear, decisive, positive, and tenacious. Practice feeling these ways. Practice having this mindset.

Mindset is everything.

#34
DON'T GET BACKED IN THE CORNER, AND WHEN YOU DO, KNOW HOW TO GET OUT

They call it the rope-a-dope. Well, I'm the dope. Ali just laid on the rope and I, like a dope, kept punching until I got tired. But he was probably the most smart fighter I've gotten in the ring with.
— George Foreman

I've got to take the measured steps and avoid the pitfalls. Life in general has pitfalls, but being a boxer there's even more.
— Daniel Dubois

There is always a solution. When you find yourself stuck, do not think about how to get out; begin with changing your state, the stuck state. You need to move and change your physiology. Movement is medicine. Then once you get moving and your happy juices and endorphins get flowing, change your story.

Boxers fight in a ring that is squared, so there are four corners and nowhere to escape. They train to get out of situations when they are backed into a corner. Boxers always know their exit plans in every moment. They learn to play the corner, how to work with the trap of getting backed into it, and all the possible ways they can get out and turn things around for their benefit.

Success leaves clues. See what other successful people in similar situations do and have done in the past, and learn what is needed to move forward and get out of the corner as quickly, efficiently, and effectively as possible. There is always a way. We have a sign on the wall in my gym that says, "Some find an excuse, others find a way." Be one of the ones that finds a way, be like a boxer, and always know your exit plan in every moment. I love the philosophy of Bruce Lee's Jeet Kune Do, which is, "Using no way as way and having no limitation as limitation." That is so beautiful.

Don't get backed into a corner, and when you do, know how to get out.

#35
KEEP IT IN THE RING

Sports are sports.
It's all about how we carry ourselves out of the ring.
— George Foreman

It would be hard to throw a punch to someone who wasn't
a boxer, who wasn't in the ring, and who didn't have on a
pair of boxing gloves and who hadn't been training.
— George Foreman

When I was a schoolteacher, I taught alternative education, and I also taught in detention centers and jails. I always said, "The jails are full because people are treated unfairly." Play fair. Be fair. Learn to not take your emotions that are related to an experience to the next experience and ruin your moments by getting stuck in an upset state. That is one of the beautiful things about boxing. Boxers learn to fight, so they do not fight. The best fighters are never angry. They are trained warriors. Boxing instills discipline and makes them humble. Boxers get clear that the *real* opponent they are always fighting is themselves. Boxers keep it in the ring, and do not carry grudges or anger afterward, outside the ring. They know it is just a job, and whatever happens in the ring, stays there.

Keep it in the ring.

#36
KNOW WHEN TO PIVOT

To be successful in life you must get in the habit
of turning negatives into positives.
— George Foreman

Like Kenny Rogers says, "You got to know when to hold 'em, know when to fold 'em, know when to walk away, know when to run." When things are not going in the direction you want, you need to notice beforehand and pivot. Do not change the goal; change the direction or actions to get there. Be adaptable and go with the flow.

Pivot. All that matters is that things work, and when whatever you are doing is not working, you need to change, or pivot. Try a new direction, new scenery—something new to get better results.

In boxing, when boxers are not comfortable, their opponents are very strong and powerful, and the opponents are using strength to push the boxers back, the boxers being pushed back would pivot. This would allow them to cancel out the strength of their opponents by deflecting their line of attack without having to retreat. Pivoting also allows the fighters to control their environment. When you change the way you look at things, the things you look at change. Sometimes a shift, move, change, hinge, or pivot is all it takes to change everything in the desirable direction.

Know when to pivot.

#37
STYLES MAKE FIGHTS

You'd have to say the cleverest fighter in boxing is Mayweather.
He adapts his style against whatever opponent he faces.
— Ricky Hatton

I had an exciting style, I was aggressive, a body
puncher, and I attacked all the time.
— Ricky Hatton

Fighting styles are what keep boxing so interesting and create upsets and more excitement for the spectators and the gamblers. Because styles make fights, anybody can potentially win or beat anyone else, regardless of their skill or performance differences with their opponents.

Boxers need to train for the fight with the specific fighter they are fighting, as every opponent is different. Due to different styles, boxers never truly know with whom they are getting in the ring, which keeps things exciting and unpredictable. It is what keeps everything interesting in the sport of boxing. Their styles are their own individual flairs and spins on their performance and executions. Elements of styles are observable behaviors. A one-style-fits-all philosophy limits potential. Fighters create styles based on their size, build, strengths, rhythm, and tempo. Just like Darwin's theory of evolution, only the strong survive; in boxing, only those with the strongest skills survive. What is so exciting is that styles make fights because a fighter's individual style can change what is an advantage and what is a disadvantage and ultimately affect the outcome when predictions were otherwise.

In life, have a style that is attractive, engaging, exciting, and able to adjust to other styles most effectively to come out the winner. Stand out, put your own flair on things, and be noticeable and unique for the benefit of your own success.

Styles make fights.

#38
THE PEOPLE IN YOUR CORNER
HELP MAKE YOU A
CHAMPION OR NOT

Boxing is individual although there is a team concept,
because you need a great corner, you need a great trainer,
you need a great prep man, you need all these things.
— Sugar Ray Leonard

All those around me are the bridge to my success, so they are all important.
— Manny Paquiao

When the trainer talks to the fighter, there's a
connection. You don't always have to say much.
— Sugar Ray Leonard

You have to trust in the people you have around you. Support and guidance are needed. Even though boxers need to see everything, their corner people are very important. They can see what the boxer's opponent is setting up when the fighter may not be able to see. They also provide feedback and help the fighter cool down and focus in between rounds. Different boxers require different things from their corners. Some need motivation, and others want detailed feedback. A good corner will know what the fighter needs and provide it.

That is what is needed in your life to be a champion. You need an objective set of eyes and perceptions that is focused on your best interests. Your team, or corner, can make or break you. You for sure want a team that makes all the difference in your performance and results. Consistent, helpful, contributive feedback is needed. You do better and get better results with people in your corner who are only after your win too, versus not having a corner at all. It all comes down to whether fighters will listen to their corners or not, though, because if they are not listening, it does not matter what is being said. The perfect team matched to the fighter is what is needed and most optimal for a fighter to become a champion. Corner people are in less-stressful positions, so they can think more clearly. They also really know their fighters, their power level, how much more their fighters can give, how they can recover from a setback, how to motivate them when needed, and when it is necessary to change the plan. When things are not working for the fighters, they can see it and explain objectively.

In life, which people you have in your corner is very important. They can make or break you. Why not set yourself up for success and have all you need to excel and win in whatever endeavor you are pursing? Get people in your corner whom you respect and honor and will listen to, as it may just be the key to your victory.

The people in your corner help make you a champion or not.

#39
DON'T BE PREDICTABLE

*When you don't change up a lot, people may
know you a lot better than they should.*
— Evander Holyfield

I always feel like there's no fighter that I can't figure out.
— Roy Jones Jr.

Assumption is the mother of the screw-ups.
— Angelo Dundee

Routine is the enemy. That is a concept I trademarked in fitness, RITE Fitness. I always say, "The moments between the notes create the music. Never have the same timing, rhythm, or tempo." Boxers never want to be predictable. If they are, they lose, as their opponents know just how to figure them out and win. Mix things up like boxers do. Do not be mundane. Do not be predictable, which is not to be confused with being consistent. Be consistent, just be exciting and different. Do not show all your cards. Always have leverage, and

    Don't be predictable.

#40
BE FIRST, BE BRAVE, AND
HAVE COURAGE

He who is not courageous enough to take risks
will accomplish nothing in life.
— Muhammad Ali

Choose to take risks. Do not wait for proof. If you feel the desire in your heart, go for it. Act on it. Do not wait. There is a sign in my gym that says, "Do today what others won't, so tomorrow you can do what others can't." Do not hit the regret stage and then wish for what you would have had if you had taken risks.

Be first. Be brave. Have courage. People who are brave and have courage do not lack fear. They have the fear, but they push through it and do it anyway. Do not delay.

What do you have to give up about yourself or move out of your way to be first, to be brave now, and to have courage? Nothing in life without risk is worthwhile. You must be relentless. That is a winner's quality. If you want to be an anomaly, you need to act like one.

Boxers know that it is important to be first. They want to be the aggressor. Boxers are obviously super brave and have courage, as they risk their lives almost daily by fighting toe to toe with their opponents. The shortest distance between two points is a straight line. All other paths are longer. Get there the quickest and smartest. That is why boxers punch in straight lines—they want to get to their opponents in the fastest way. Boxers' reach is always shown on the TV for their fights, as every inch they have over their opponents is an advantage.

I am a pragmatist, so I do what works, not what does not work. Push yourself out of your comfort zone. Do things that require you to have courage and be brave. Courage breeds confidence. Like Nike says, "Just do it." I say, "Do it *now*, while the moment is hot and the thought about it is there, alive and real." Do what works. Fear may be present. That's ok. *Feel* the fear and do it anyway.

Be first. Be brave. Have courage.

#41
PRAY, HAVE FAITH, AND BELIEVE IN A HIGHER POWER

With God, hard work and focus I can accomplish
what is ahead of me.
— Manny Paquiao

Prayer is a method practiced from ancient days,
so it's very important for us to maintain a spiritual
connection, something that people, gladiators would do
years ago so we're just maintaining that routine.
— Anthony Joshua

I have a tattoo that says "Ho'oponopono." To me, it is the only prayer you need: "I'm sorry. Please forgive me. Thank you. I love you."

I pray, I have faith, and I believe in a higher power. There is an intelligence that is giving us life—a higher power, unexplainable, all-knowing intelligence. I know we come from this source, which is a unified consciousness of only love. I pray *as* source *to* source. We are all *from* this source. It is in us and all around us.

Boxers are always thanking God, Jesus, Allah, and whomever else they believe helped get them to where they are. Boxers pray, have faith, and believe in a higher power. Most boxers pray in their corners prior to the bell ringing, and they also thank God and whomever else they worship and believe in after the fight is over as well. They know they did not get to where they are all alone. Boxers have faith they will come out of the ring the same way they walked in it, and they have faith they will prevail.

Faith is imagination directed. Fear is the opposite—imagination undirected. Have faith. Be directed. You are God's child, and through God *all* things are possible. I am clear that something greater than me is in charge of my destiny and fate. I am a universal citizen. In God, I move and breathe and have my being. My every attempt in life is to be in that space and to live in it. I live in the breath that is God and allow the breath to breathe me as God. This allows me to grow in grace and all that is offered to me in that space. Our lives are always talking to us. We must listen. Life and God are always speaking to us. Be silent enough to hear. Pay attention to everything.

Pray. Have faith. Believe in a higher power.

#42
BE POSITIVE

I'm one of the most optimistic persons in the world.
I always believed that there's another shot, another chance. In boxing, I
never gave up. I kept trying, kept trying. Even when things seemed so dim,
I continued to push forward to make something happen in my favor.
— Sugar Ray Leonard

Don't count the days, make the days count.
— Muhammad Ali

There is never, ever, ever, ever a reason to have a disempowering mindset. Why not be positive? It only makes the situation better. Nothing productive comes from negativity except the awareness that positivity is missing and needs to be put in place. It is not the facts that make you miserable; it is your own perception of the facts that make you miserable.

Boxers are positive, and they empower themselves to feel good and believe they will win even when no one else does. They do not let negativity get in the way as they know they cannot win with a negative mindset. They have a clear, positive, mental attitude, and they know it is needed to have a successful boxing career.

Get good at cheering for yourself and turning down the volume of the voices in your head. Hear the voices. It is okay to feel overwhelmed, doubtful, or like an impostor—*but* it is what you do with that energy that matters. Transfer and transform that energy. Make the empowering and positive voices louder and mute the negative chatter.

Name the positive part of yourself, and then call that part forward when needed. Have rituals that add to your life. Do things that make you feel positive. Think things that make you feel positive. Notice when you are not feeling and thinking positively. Do not resist it; just notice it, allow it, and *let that shit go. Choose to be positive and practice feeling good.* A winning mindset is positive. Be like a boxer and cultivate a positive attitude and outlook. It aligns with winning.

Be positive.

#43
HAVE PATIENCE

Having patience is one of the hardest things about
being human. We want to do it now,
and we don't want to wait. Sometimes we miss out on our blessing
when we rush things and do it on our own time.
— Deontay Wilder

Don't worry about the title. Worry about what you got to do today,
tomorrow, the next day and the title will be waiting for you.
— Anthony Joshua

Life is never about what happens to us. It is always about how we react, respond, feel, think, perceive, combine, and stack those things that happen to us. Patience is the ability to accept delay without getting upset. It is the understanding that there is a process to everything. Boxers have long, hard journeys. They have to be like white on rice with their craft. They must be patient, as experience mostly wins, and they need to pay their dues big time. I always get upset and think it is disrespectful when people in their late twenties and older come into my boxing gym and say they want to fight professionally. I always say, "That's like coming in and saying you want to be Tiger Woods." Boxing is not easy, and getting to the top is not a quick journey. It is for sure a journey of more than a thousand miles, and in order to be groomed, as a champion is, a boxer needs to start early, train always, fight often, and be patient—just how we want to be *in life*.

We need to first be patient with ourselves, and then we can in turn be patient with others and the world around us. What is the rush? I say to myself, *I have all the time in the world*, I breathe deeply and fully, and I center myself into the generous, present moment. It makes me feel so good. Worrying and lacking patience do nothing to help a process, and they bring nothing good or positive to the situation. Lacking patience is just not what works. I am a pragmatist. Practice what works and get rid of what does not work. It sounds easy and it can be, but it may not be. Either way it is a practice. Notice when you have patience. How do you feel? Always notice your breath. When you are relaxed, so is your breath. When you are not relaxed and you are overwhelmed, worried, or impatient, your breath is shorter. You are then living by the hormones of stress. Nothing good is there, so have patience. Be patient. Practice being patient, just like a boxer. Do your best and trust the process.

Have patience.

#44
NEVER TURN YOUR BACK

I learned to run backwards from Muhammad Ali. He told me about running backwards because you try to imitate everything you do in the ring, so sometimes you back-up.
— Sugar Ray Leonard

Always look forward. How can you see what is in front of you if you have your back turned? You cannot. Just like boxers frequently do in their fights, you too can pivot, you can step back, and you can pivot to a side to change the scenery, but do not turn your back. You cannot protect yourself when you are not facing what is attacking you. You always want to see what is in front of you and not give your back to the life that is happening in front of you. You will get clocked in a boxing match and in life. Turning your back only makes everything worse. It is just something you do not do. In boxing, it is considered an illegal blow to hit an opponent in the back of the head, and the referee will warn the fighter to not turn his or her back as well. In boxing it is a no-no for both parties. Do not hit on the back of the head, and never turn your back. In life, when walking away is not your best option, you are in the line of fire, or you need to be fully on, *never turn your back*. You need to face whatever is in front of you head-on, face-forward. Go through the storm to get out of it instead of turning your back because it will blow you over and kill you.

Never turn your back.

#45
TRUST THE PROCESS:
SURRENDER

Just take one step at a time, trusting that God still has a plan
for you, and He will make the best out of your situation.
— George Foreman

Surrender does not mean to give up. *Surrender* means to give over to God, the universe. Continue to take action, yet trust the process and *know* that everything is always working out for you. It has in the past, and it will continue to do so. Like a boxer, give it your all. Lay all you have on the table and fight your heart out. Sometimes it is just not your night or is not meant to be. Boxers still believe in themselves, and they keep coming back as they surrender to the process while still believing they will triumph. Know that life is happening *for* you, not *to* you. Stay in constant action, do the right things and the next right things, and then surrender to and trust the process, just like a boxer does.

When you do the right thing, act from your heart, live in light, align yourself with yourself, and trust that all works out in your favor as designed, and as you design, all works out for you. The universe hooks you up; just trust and surrender. No need to force it. Let it all unfold. Allow. Meditate. Behave in manners that are conducive to your future self and know that you are becoming all you are creating yourself to be. I always say, "The moment between the notes create the music." Live in your music, surrender, and *live life in the now*—and then in the *now*, and then in the *now*. Life is generated moment by moment, and manifestation happens at the speed of surrender.

Trust the process. Surrender.

#46
DRESS HOW YOU WANT
TO BE PERCEIVED

I always designed my robes and how I would present myself at every fight.
— Sugar Ray Leonard

Create the person you want the world to see. Impressions and presentations are everything. People see, people judge, and people create stories in their heads. We humans have brains that are just meaning-making machines. Show the world how you want to be seen. Present yourself in such a way that is aligned with who you are and who you want to become. Thought becomes form. Show the world what to think.

Do you want to be influential? In what ways? The way you dress, the way you talk, the way you think, and your capacity for learning are all ways you can influence. If there is a skill needed, you can get it. If something needs to be learned, you can learn it. Dress for success.

Boxers have so much fun making their shorts, robes, jackets, and corner people uniforms. They become recognizable by their entrance and attire. They dress how they want to be perceived. The way boxers enter the ring and their style precedes them.

Dress to impress. Why not? *Be your brand.* I have always loved to live in gym clothes. I created my life to live that way. I am fortunate as I own a gym and am in the health and fitness industry, so I always get to wear fun, comfy gym clothes. They satisfy my desire for freedom and comfort and at the same time represent who I am in the world and my brand. No one has ever had to guess what industry I am in when I walk into a room.

Dress how you want to be perceived.

#47
FEEL—
YOU NEED TO MOURN

You need to mourn, you need to be upset, to give yourself time to replenish.
Then you use it all as fuel to get stronger.
— Anthony Yarde

You would not know amazing if you did not know terrible. We live in a world of contrast and polarity, and then we seek balance. Feel your emotions so they can pass, as things we resist persist. If you do not want something to persist, then do not resist its existence and presence. Once you mourn and allow yourself to feel sad, or whatever the unwanted emotion is, then you can pass through it. Whatever goes up must come down, so do not fight gravity, and that which is.

You cannot avoid or ignore things and expect them to go away. I say that is like having cherries on top of shit pie. You cannot create anew with "stuff" in the space, as creation comes from nothing, not something. You need to acknowledge and *feel* the emotions you are feeling, *allow* them in, *allow* them to pass through you, and recognize them for what they are—just emotions, energy in motion. When I am sad, I say, "So this is sad. I am sad. I'm going to be sad right now." And I do. I immerse myself in the emotion, and then it goes away. It does not get buried; it passes. Another important and great practice is meditation. Having a daily practice is so good for you. It allows you to become most familiar with yourself and have things pass and move through you, not confine you. It allows you to exist and immerse yourself in the generous, present moment.

Boxers have high highs and low lows, and they feel immensely. Floyd Patterson described how he felt after losing in the *Ali: King of the World* book, saying he just wished he could leave through a trap door in the middle of the ring and escape from the crowds. Then, when boxers win, they are on top of the world. It is for sure an emotional roller coaster, like life is, but boxers roll with the punches. They are very present, feel whatever is present, and move on, as we want to do *in life*.

Practice feeling good so that when you are down, you can feel down and get out of it quickly with your worked muscles and various practices on how to feel good. When you are feeling good, notice you are feeling good and have gratitude. Work on staying in these elevated emotions as long as possible. It is a practice, and we get good at things we practice over and over again. Get good at allowing yourself to mourn and be sad when you are, and then get good at feeling good once it passes. It is always about the comeback, not the setback. So mourn what needs to be mourned, and then come back stronger.

Feel! You need to mourn.

JOLIE
G
J
GLASSMAN

#48
TIMING IS EVERYTHING

Not only do I knock them out ... but I pick the round.
— Muhammad Ali

We often hear timing is everything, yet do we plan and train to time things perfectly? Do we believe and know that we can time things as we want them to show up for ourselves and our lives? Timing is a skill or the action of judging the right moment to execute something in any given situation.

Do not wait for the right time; create and find the right time and capitalize on it. Time things to win. People and their actions have patterns. Notice them beforehand and time things accordingly to best accomplish what you are setting out to achieve. Timing beats speed. In the ring and in life, we all need to know exactly when and where to hit the target. Boxers need to come out jabbing, and when they measure the correct distance to their target and the timing is right, they can throw their power punches and connect. If you miss the right time, you miss out on the opportunity. You have to do the right things at the right time; otherwise, it is not right and does not work. Do not plant in the wintertime or you will lose out. Everything has its time and moment— the key is to tune in and align your timing with the opportunity you want to land, just like a boxer.

Timing is everything.

#49
MUST BE PRESENT AT ALL TIMES

All the time he's boxing, he's thinking. All the time
he was thinking, I was hitting him.
— Jack Dempsey

Presence is one of the cornerstones of the Zen tradition of Buddhism, in which monks work for years to develop the stillness and sharpness of mind to do only one thing at a time. Most of the time, we do one thing while thinking of something else, or we even do three things at the same time, such as talking on the phone, folding laundry, and cooking. There is nothing inherently wrong with multitasking, which seems necessary at times, especially in the midst of family life. However, balancing this with a healthy dose of activity done with intentional presence can provide valuable insight into the benefits of doing one thing at a time and being fully present with whatever the task at hand happens to be. Be present. How can you focus and fully be somewhere if your mind is somewhere else? You cannot. Work on presence and doing what you are doing when you are doing it. Get out of the habit of thinking of what you are going to say and do next, as you can do that when you get there. Become one with what you are doing. The present moment is where all wisdom is revealed and where performance is at its best.

Boxers can never box without being present, not even for a millisecond. They will get knocked out. There are no time-outs in boxing, and during the one minute they do have in the corner after each round finishes, they are getting yelled at and having their cuts tended to and cleaned up quickly just in time for the bell to ring and for them to get back in there for more fighting. Boxers train to be present and on at all times. Like boxers, we all need to practice being present at all times. The only time to be "off" is when we are resting or sleeping; otherwise, there is no time for rest. Everyday is an opportunity to create a living masterpiece. You need to always be your best, and being your best requires presence. Be where you are. Where else are you going? You physically cannot be in two places at once, so do not try to be. Nothing else exists except the now. *Be here now*, unless you are dreaming—then be there. Wherever you are, *be there* fully. Get to know the generous present moment. You can train for it just like boxers do.

Be present at all times.

#50
ALWAYS BE READY

The same hand that can write a beautiful poem
can knock you out with one punch—
that's poetic justice.
— "Irish" Wayne Kelly

Prepare yourself to always be ready. The more you are prepared, the more value you get out of what is coming your way. Be well equipped to be really valuable. When you anticipate crisis, change will be a gift. Fitness is a state of readiness. When you are fit, you are ready. Every day, push your body. Train yourself not to hesitate. Say, "One, two, three, *go*" or whatever your pattern is to make things happen most effectively and fastest, and then go with *no negotiation. Train yourself to do that.*

Romeo, the head boxing trainer at my South Beach Boxing gym, always says, "Always be ready, so you don't have to get ready." Boxers need to always be ready and always be in shape, especially if they want to be champions. Sometimes a fight comes up that they cannot refuse. They must be ready. I always say the hardest thing for a professional athlete is to be on when someone says so, at any given moment. We all have good days and bad days, yet boxers need to be ready and on at all times, whether they feel like it or not. Boxers who train to be champions are always ready to go, whenever.

Train in life to always be ready. Always be preparing so that you never need to prepare, as then you are always ready for whatever comes your way.

Always be ready.

#51
PREPARE FOR THE UNEXPECTED

I always expect challenges. Boxing is not an easy sport.
— Sugar Ray Leonard

Always expect challenges. If you did not have them, you would be dead, as life is filled with consistent challenges; therefore, do not let them shock or surprise you. If everything were easy, we would all have everything. It is the struggle you push through that brings you the success. Anticipation is power. Leaders anticipate; losers react. Know the road ahead.

Boxing is not an easy sport. Boxers prepare for the unexpected. Because styles make fights and they never truly know who they are getting in the ring with, they need to prepare for any and all possibilities and not leave themselves open to surprises. Boxers plan, prepare, and train for the unexpected. We want to do that in life too. Know the pitfalls and what others have gone through in the past in the same or similar situations. Do not make unnecessary mistakes that could have been avoided with preparation for whatever comes your way.

Prepare for the unexpected.

#52
PLAY BIG

I want to be the best. Not just the best fighter. I want
to be the best athlete, period. When I leave, I will
be known as TBE and that's The Best Ever.
— Floyd Mayweather Jr.

We often hear "go hard or go home." Exactly. What is the point of playing if you are not playing big? You only live once. This is not a dress rehearsal. We definitely do not want to do things in life or have habits that we will regret later. We are here to manifest ourselves into our greatest potential. Do we even know what that is? Play so big that you discover and grow into the best version of yourself. So what if you fail? You cannot succeed at things if you do not fail along the way. Failing is part of the journey, and it is not a destination unless you give up. Dream big and then play big. If your dreams do not scare you, then you are not dreaming big enough. No one is getting out alive, and only one thing will ultimately kill you, so we might as well live out our wildest dreams and play full out in life. Boxing is a one-on-one sport, and to be a champion who is recognized at the top of the game, boxers have to play big. Do that in life.

Play big.

#53
APPRECIATE—
HAVE GRATITUDE

*Everything I have in this world, I owe to the sport
of boxing, and I won't ever forget that.*
— Oscar De La Hoya

*I consider myself blessed. I consider you blessed. We've
all been blessed with God-given talents.*
— Sugar Ray Leonard

The only prayer ever needed is "Thank you." Choose to get up every day and bless your day. Give thanks. Though you have no idea what will happen, you can know it is blessed. Just because you are alive, say, "This day in my life will never come again. I will never see this … or this … nothing like this will ever come again. I am grateful." Live in gratitude. Appreciate the little things, and then the little things will become big things. Recognize the full worth of something, as the palace of happiness rests on the grounds of gratitude.

Gratitude is the greatest state of receivership. It is the door to abundance. It is feeling as if the event has already occurred. Cultivate gratitude. Practice having gratitude. What you put out will come back. So give thanks, and you will receive more to be thankful for.

Gratitude *is* the way. You are who you practice to be. If you practice gratitude, you are grateful. Gratitude is the cure to anger. There is no pain in gratitude, only joy and appreciation. You cannot think greater than you feel, so feel greater and then think greater.

Boxers are filled with gratitude. They know that aside from their faith in their higher power, they owe everything they have to the sport of boxing. They know that they are blessed and have God-given talents.

Every day, review who you want to be and who you no longer want to be. Then become elevated in your emotions that you feel when you are being who you want to be. Your thoughts carry information, they carry frequency, and they send out signals, and then your feelings and emotions bring the events back to you. If you feel great and are filled with gratitude, more things will come your way that align with that feeling; and if you feel terrible, angry, and resentful, more things will come your way that align with those feelings. So how would you rather feel? We humans differ from animals in that we have the power to choose, and we are always choosing, whether we recognize it or not. Where focus goes, energy flows. So focus on your abundance, and be grateful. Choose to be appreciative and grateful, and see how great your life looks, feels, and unfolds. Spend time investing in your heart. Your brain thinks; your heart knows. Cultivate and align both. They either are coherent or are not.

Living in a state of gratitude allows us to spread our abundance because that is the energy we emanate. The universe wants to shower us with blessings. The more we appreciate life, the more life appreciates and delivers us more goodness.

Appreciate. Have gratitude.

JOLIE
GLASSMAN

#54
DON'T WORRY ABOUT
WHAT OTHERS ARE DOING

I don't need to worry about what other people are talking about me. Instead, I focus on the people talking positive and all the positive things that I know I am doing.
— Anthony Yarde

Comparison is the thief of all joy. When you spend your time focusing on other people, you give them energy over you. You give them power. Where focus goes, energy flows. You do not want to spend your energy and attention on what other people are saying about you. Instead, you want to focus on the people talking positively and all the positive things you know you are doing. Worry alone takes you off your game, and nothing positive or advantageous comes from it. Learn to focus on yourself and not what others are doing.

Boxers are always focused on their own training and the road ahead of them. To boxers, others are just those they need to beat along the way. Boxers are clear that worrying is a waste of time, and they really just focus on growing themselves into the best versions of themselves. That is what we all need to do, and therefore all focus needs to be on ourselves, who we are being, and what we are doing. Do not believe in competition. There is enough for all of us. Do not view anyone in your industry as a competitor but more as a soul sister or brother who also has come here to serve. There is only one you, and that is your superpower. Do not give up your power focusing on what others are doing. Instead utilize your power to focus, and do what you are doing and needing to do to accomplish all your heart desires.

Don't worry about what others are doing.

#55

BE VIGILANT,
KEEP YOUR HANDS UP,
AND PROTECT YOURSELF AT ALL TIMES

Everyone has a plan 'til they get punched in the face.
— Mike Tyson

Be vigilant. Be wary. Keep your hands up and protect yourself at all times—this is one of the most popular, well-known rules of boxing. You always want to be able to protect and defend yourself. Boxers keep their hands up to protect themselves from getting hit in the face and vital organs of the body.

It is very important in life to protect ourselves and know how to defend ourselves. We definitely do not want to get caught blindsided and have regrets. It is better to protect and defend ourselves against viruses, negative energy, negative people and dealings, and bad situations in advance, before they attack us and get the better of us.

Learn how to defend yourself in many ways against many things—not to be in fear of them but to be empowered in your defenses against them. Knowledge is potential power; gather it up and use it accordingly.

Be vigilant. Keep your hands up and protect yourself at all times.

#56

BALANCE IS EVERYTHING

Focus on being balanced—success is balance.
— Laila Ali

Boxers always stay grounded and keep their feet directly underneath them. They do not let their bodies come over the front of their feet. Balance is everything. It is an even distribution of weight enabling something to stand up strong and steady. Without balance, things fall apart. Focus on being balanced. If boxers are off balance, they can get knocked out easily. Boxers can never lose their balance in any circumstance. They train for balance and focus on having it as a number-one priority, as without it, they will never win. Seek balance. Train for balance. Be balanced. Live a balanced life.

I see and hear people say, "Balance is bullshit." I for sure do not want to learn from them. To me life is always how you see it and what you make it. You want to make balance in your life, not bullshit. Many people have and exist in balance, and those are the people you want to emulate in those ways. Ask them questions to see how they achieve it and what they do. If you believe balance is bullshit, you will live an imbalanced life. You get what you tolerate. If you make balance a priority and a must, you will live balanced. It is all about your priorities and what you make a "must do" versus a "should do." Notice when things are out of balance. It is not a good feeling, and there are many ways to get and achieve balance. Have routines that serve you, stabilize you, and help you create balance in your life. Know your needs and give them to yourself, as being centered and balanced and feeling good and stable are super important. Therefore, live accordingly.

I recommend daily meditation, silence, music, breath work, Pilates, stretching, coloring, a morning routine that serves you, a nighttime turn-down routine, a gratitude practice, having a pet, being outdoors, exercising, doing things you love, serving, contributing, and boxing, of course. Challenge yourself. Balance in the body is neurological. You can train yourself to be balanced; just practice it. Stand on one leg and close your eyes, and then practice unlimited variations to test and build your balance. Know when you feel balanced and when you do not. Just saying the word *balanced* feels good.

Seek balance, know that it is not bullshit. It is not easy, yet if it is something you want, know that it is certainly possible to have it when you prioritize it, make it a must, and honor yourself enough to establish boundaries that maintain your balance. We are all the boss of ourselves. Love yourself enough to live a balanced life. Stay strong, steady, and even; you are the boss of yourself. Having balance is not to be confused with having less and limiting beliefs on what is possible. It is all how you make it and interpret it, yet having balance is not an either-or proposition. You can still have it all and have balance. Study those who are, do, and have what you are after and ask lots of questions so you can achieve balance in the areas where you feel you are off balance. Remember, balance is everything. *You got this*!

Live life like a boxer, follow all these rules, and you will have balance. Be the badass of your own life and your own story. *Be, do, and have balance.*

Balance is everything.

JOLIE
G
GLASSMAN

#57

REMEMBER WHERE YOU CAME FROM, AND IT DOESN'T HAVE TO BE WHERE YOU'RE GOING

I remember as a little boy I ate one meal a day and sometimes slept in the street. I will never forget that, and it inspires me to fight hard, stay strong, and remember all the people of my country, trying to achieve better for themselves.
— Manny Paquiao

When people see what I have now, they have no idea where I came from and how I didn't have anything growing up.
— Floyd Mayweather Jr.

Be humble in the journey that got you to where you are heading. Always remember where you came from and know it has nothing to do with how far you can go in life. Boxing is such a beautiful sport; I compare boxers to lotus flowers. Just like boxers, lotus flowers bloom most magnificently from the thickest and deepest mud. Many boxers come from the streets or poor backgrounds, and have had to learn to fight to be able to eat and have a roof over their heads. They have fought for their lives. They came from nothing and then grew into professional athletes who are world renowned. Boxing is a dirty sport filled with corrupt managers, promoters, judges, sanctioning bodies, and so on, but the boxers are the beautiful lotus flowers that grow from the muddy surroundings and upbringings. To become a champion and embody all these rules, you want to remember where you came from, everything that got you to where you are, and where you are headed. Let those things drive you and continue to push you forward in the direction of your desires.

Your past does not equal your future unless you live there. Do not live where you do not want to be. Become the lotus flower. What matters is where you are now and where you are going, not where you came from. Yet never forget it, as your story of struggle makes you the champ in your own life. If my mom was the mother I hoped she would be, I would not be the woman I *am*. God gave me exactly what I needed to be me, and therefore, I thank my mom every day, and I choose my mom for all the good, bad, and ugly.

Let us all be like lotus flowers and create beautiful colors and life-forms from thick, deep mud, just as boxers do. Turn lemons into lemonade.

Remember where you came from, and it doesn't have to be where you're going.

#58
FIND AND CREATE OPENINGS

Within our dreams and aspirations we find our opportunities.
— Sugar Ray Leonard

If you keep knocking you will find open doors, and if there is no door, make a door. You do not have to close one door for another one to open. There are never-ending possibilities and openings; you just need to seek and find them. Finding is reserved for the searchers. Seek and you will find, as if you do not seek, you for sure will not find. Rarely will a good idea interrupt you.

Boxers are constantly looking for openings in the guard of their opponent. Boxing is all about angles and finding and creating openings to get in on their opponents, and break them down or knock them out. The opponents block, defend, and cover themselves up as best as they can, and the goal is to find or otherwise create an opening to attack with precision, power, and speed and then get out with their jabs and do it all again for the duration of the fight.

Be the boxer in your life—find and create openings and opportunities for great setups and future moves. Be the fighter in life. Take charge. Find and seek openings, create opportunities, knock open doors, make new doors, and do whatever it takes to be the winning boxer, or fighter, in your life.

Find and create openings.

#59
MAKE YOURSELF COMFORTABLE
WITH THE UNCOMFORTABLE

Boxing is the ultimate challenge. There's nothing that can compare to testing yourself the way you do every time you step in the ring.
— Sugar Ray Leonard

Boxing is the ultimate challenge. It is not a comfortable situation, nor is it expected to be. The two in the ring are in a fight and an extreme workout, to say the least, pushing past limits they did not even know they had to push. Boxers get used to it. There is no comfort in boxing other than knowing that it is consistently uncomfortable and then finding comfort in the knowing and the expectation of it. When things get uncomfortable, which is almost all the time, boxers do not get surprised or rocked or show they are uncomfortable. They are actually used to it and know it is all part of the game. They become comfortable with the uncomfortable because it is commonplace and is to be expected. They practice being uncomfortable to the point that it becomes comfortable. Being uncomfortable is not a trait for winning.

Growth comes from stepping out of your comfort zone. Get used to how things really are so you can just relax into it and get comfortable with that which is inevitable, rendering it no longer uncomfortable. Get comfortable with the way things are and what you cannot change, as that is the way it is. How you deal with it and approach it is all that matters. One way to measure success is to look at how uncomfortable you were able to get and therefore were forced to grow. Those who do not think outside the box are easily contained.

I have a sign on my front door with a quote from Eckhart Tolle: "Accept then act. Whatever the present moment contains, accept it as if you had chosen it. Always work with it, not against it. Make it your friend and ally, not your enemy. This will miraculously transform your whole life."

Boxers are in positions that are extremely uncomfortable. They step in the ring, put it all on the line, and take the challenge of settling into comfort during the ultimate challenge of discomfort. They make the uncomfortable comfortable.

How would you rather feel, comfortable or uncomfortable? That is a rhetorical question. Of course, you would rather feel comfortable. So practice.

Get used to uncomfortable situations, as that is life. Expect them and get comfortable with them, as discomfort is a part of life. Resisting what is just lets it persist. Comfort is a place of power compared to discomfort, which is not a place of power. Always stand in power, comfortably, no matter what.

Make yourself comfortable with the uncomfortable.

JOLIE
GLASSMAN

#60
FIGHT YOUR HEART OUT—
BOXERS ARE ALL HEART

A champion is someone who gets up when he can't.
— Jack Dempsey

Boxers fight their hearts out and are all heart. To win in boxing and become a champion, you need to get up when you cannot. There are always upsets in boxing. Things can always turn around, and boxers cannot just give up when they are tired, feel beat up, or think they cannot fight anymore. If they want to continue and win, they need to fight their hearts out, despite any obstacle, because the fight is not over until someone gets knocked out or the bell of the final round rings.

Heart is the ability to keep swinging and punching when there is nothing left to recharge the body and then continuing to fight with great vigor and intensity to the point of exhaustion, and beyond.

Boxing gyms are where kids and adults go to save themselves. They come from adversity and pain and rise to the occasion to overcome themselves. They fight their hearts out. Fight always. Fight for what you believe in and for what is right, and always fight from your heart. Ask yourself, *What would God do? What would Jesus do? What would my heart do?* Do that.

Who you are is in your heart. Where you live is in your head. *Cultivate both.* Lead and come from your heart, yet take your brain with you. The brain thinks, and the heart knows. Our hearts are the bridge to oneness, the seat of the soul. Live from the heart and be one with it. When you come from your heart, not your head, anything is possible in your relationships and in your life. So love with all your heart, be with all your heart, and be the champion boxer of your own life.

Fight your heart out as boxers are all heart.

#61
BE AN AMAZING
PROBLEM SOLVER

There's one thing I don't ever think about: losing.
Instead, I think about how I'm going to win,
and how I can do it the quickest way.
— Joe Frazier

Approach problem solving by keeping in mind the problem you are solving and being intentional and purposeful about it. Like the saying goes, "Never take your eye off the ball." Follow the clues to the prize.

Boxers are constantly facing problems and solving them head-on while at the same time bumping into many more problems to solve. Boxers are amazing problem solvers. They practice, learn, prepare, study, and imagine as many possible reactions to many different scenarios for the specific fighter they are fighting. They find a way quickly, in the moment, on the fly, or they can get knocked out. Boxers solve problems like whack-a-mole pros.

In fact, life is like playing whack-a-mole; therefore, be like a boxer in life, and be an amazing problem solver. People's biggest problem is they think they are not supposed to have problems. But they are what change the world. From problems come opportunity and creation and growth. People try to avoid them at all costs even though they are unavoidable. Solving problems takes philosophy and strategy, as what you think, what you believe, and your order of actions create your whole life.

Know if what you are doing is working or not working, and act accordingly to make it all work as desired. Keep what does work, take out what does not work, and keep reassessing what else can be added or implemented to make it that much better. Solving problems is what makes you a leader. People need to learn the power and goodness of problems. The only people without problems are dead. Pray for problems as they are a sign of life and your next lesson.

Be obsessed with expanding and growing and serving. The bigger the problem is, the greater the reward will be when you solve it. Keep your eye on the desired outcome and do the right things along the way to get there. The size of the hero is determined by the size of the opponent. Have big problems worth fighting for and be the problem-solving hero of your own life. To solve a problem, you need to remove the cause, not the symptom.

Solving problems is what makes you improve and grow. Jim Rohn says, "For things to get better, you have to get better. For things to improve, you have to improve. When you grow, everything in your life grows with you. Don't wish it were easier, wish you were better."

Screw easy—*be better*. Know that being alive means having problems to solve. Welcome them. Like boxers, get worthy opponents, or problems worth fighting for, and then

Be an amazing problem solver.

148

#62
SHOW NO PAIN

A sight game is that I am hurt, but I aim to make you believe that I am not even hurt, and with this confidence appearing on my face, I don't panic otherwise your opponent will know that you are hurt. That's the whole art game in boxing.
— Evander Holyfield

Pain is inevitable, but that does not mean you have to show it or suffer from it. When I was learning Muay Thai fighting, my trainer constantly told me to show no pain, and when I did, he would smack me, yell at me, and then smack me again and again until I showed no reaction. That took a very long time and was very difficult to do. It is a practice, like just about everything else.

Remember—and I say this often—where focus goes, energy flows. Focus on the prize, not the pain. If boxers show pain, their opponents know they have 'em hurt. The opponents then have leverage and are on their way to winning. They will then know to put on extra pressure, inflict more pain, and go for the knockout. There's no need to show pain and increase your chances of losing.

Just like in boxing, pain is part of life, so just process it, move forward, and get on with it. The slogan on our gym T-shirts says, "Pain is weakness leaving the body." Just let it go, without showing its existence. Nobody needs to know about it, sometimes not even yourself. You decide what you let in or not, and either way, you do not have to demonstrate it.

Show no pain.

#63
FIGHT TO YOUR STRENGTHS: USE YOUR ASSETS, YOUR BEST TOOLS

Everybody is blessed with a certain talent, you have to know what that talent is. You have to maximize it and push it to the limit.
— Floyd Mayweather Jr.

I've always said that the best version of me can beat anyone in the world, and as long as the best version of me steps through those ropes, I can use my strengths to take away his strengths.
— Callum Smith

Fine tune your strengths because they are your assets. Know what you are good at and get greater. When I was a schoolteacher, I was always taught and encouraged to work on students' weaknesses, but I wanted to delve deeper and highlight their strengths. Once I got to run my own business and create things my way, I started to give several diagnostic strength tests to hiring candidates to see if their greatest strengths would contribute to my needs and align with my brand and mission. Once I know they will, I hire them, use them for their strengths and contributions, and constantly remind them of who they are and what strengths they have. People do better in things they are good at, and when they are reminded that they are good at something, it adds a positive vibe to their efforts. I always have such an amazing team because a chain is only as strong as its weakest link, and I never want weak links. I combine team members of great strengths, and everyone leads and contributes accordingly. My businesses operate off pure emergence, and in turn we all create magic.

Boxers need to fight to their strengths and use whatever superpowers they have to beat their opponents. They become famous for their special strengths and talents, and some of them become unbeatable for a very long time due to their strengths' being so overpowering to anyone else's strengths and assets. The greater fighter wins.

Get strong. Accumulate assets. Discover your best, related talents. Work consistently on perfecting them. Always

Fight to your strengths, and use your best assets and your best tools.

#64
ALWAYS HAVE A PLAN AND
BACK-UP PLANS AS WELL

*I play chess for about four hours a day in training camp. You have
to decide what move to use, or what combination of moves.*
— Lennox Lewis

Have a game plan and follow it. Believe in your plan, persevere, and do not get flustered at the first sign that it may not work perfectly. Put systems in place, and always be well prepared. Get ready! Prepare! Preparing beforehand and envisioning how things will go down means you are taking it seriously and thinking. Prepare yourself for success. Life does not waste success on the unprepared. Ask yourself, *What can I do to make myself ready?* Life is not designed to give us what we want or what we need. Life is designed to give us what we deserve. Those who search will find. Search! Go after it! Find it! Go where it is. It will not find you. Good ideas do not find you. Prepare, make plans, and go after all you need to accomplish. Prepare yourself to be ready for challenge, fortune, and opportunity. Opportunity passes by those who are not ready or well prepared. Ask yourself, *How can I be sharper? How can I be clearer? How can my ideas be more powerful? How can I reach people next year that I could not this year?* The more you prepare, the more you can cash in and realize more value. Be well equipped to really be valuable. Talk to yourself always.

Benjamin Franklin said, "If you fail to plan, you plan to fail."

Boxers prepare, train, and have many plans and options that they can whip out on fight night. They study their opponents, practice various combinations and moves, and they prepare consistently and extensively for their fights in order to win.

Put systems in place and follow them until you get what you want. Keep what works, get rid of what does not work, and put in what would work better. Then repeat continuously, always.

Have a plan. Be strategic. Know and visualize how you want the end to look, and plan accordingly. Have an order to things. Take one step at a time. Have direction. Create flow. Know what comes next, step by step. That is how it is done. One step at a time.

Always have a plan and back-up plans as well.

#65
DON'T LOSE FOCUS:
KEEP YOUR EYES ON THE TARGET

Keep your focus on what matters the most.
— Manny Paquiao

You always want to look forward and keep your eyes on the target. Focus, and do not lose that focus. If boxers take their eyes off the center of their opponents' chests, they are open to get knocked out, as the only punches that knock out a fighter are the ones they did not see. How can you see where you are going or what you are doing if you take your eyes off the target? You cannot. Do not get distracted. If boxers look at the ground, they just may get an uppercut to the chin. Boxers do not even blink their eyes, as that is when everything happens, in the blink of an eye. I always say boxers have to keep their eyes open in what is like a nonstop car crash. Be like a boxer, and look forward, with eyes wide opened, and do not take them off the target.

In your mind, you can transform anything with your words, integrity, and *focus*. Wherever focus goes, energy flows. Focus on the outcome and the results you want to achieve.

Don't lose focus. Keep your eyes on the target.

#66
REFUSE TO LOSE

I refuse to be beat.
— Mike Tyson

I do not lose; I just do not get decisions sometimes.
You lose when you quit. I have never quit. When it comes
down to a decision, judges make a decision as to which
fighter they want to win the fight. I have always been able to
survive no matter whom they decide to give the fight to.
— Evander Holyfield

Refuse to lose. Remove losing as an option. You win or learn. Disappointment either drives us or destroys us. Let it drive you. You can either move toward something or away from it. See the win and refuse any negative chatter and mindset. A winning attitude is what is needed to win, and winners refuse to lose.

Boxers are such heroes that when they lose a fight, they are already talking about their next fight and their comeback. Boxers train to win, plan to win, see the wins, and refuse to lose. They go all in and fully embody their own heroism. They see themselves as champions, winning the fights, and it fuels them in their training and in their fights. Do the same in your life. Go all in, embody your own heroism, see yourself as a champion, see yourself winning, and do whatever it takes.

Refuse to lose.

#67
LEARN WHO YOUR
REAL FRIENDS ARE

Everybody you fight is not your enemy, and
everybody that helps you is not your friend.
— Mike Tyson

Notice who is in your locker room after you lose,
not after you win.
— Angelo Dundee

Surround yourself with people who love and respect you and who also want to make a difference and be the change—ones who walk their talk. Always choose your friends wisely. Prefer friends who challenge you and encourage you to become the best version of yourself. Desire friends who admire and champion you as well. Know that proximity is power, and we are whom we surround ourselves with the most and spend our most precious time. Also learn to be your own best friend, and you will only accept others who align.

Boxing is a very lonely sport. When boxers win, everyone is their friend, but when they lose, that is when they learn who their real friends are. Mike Tyson told me that he tries to make his "friends" hate him, because a real friend would never. Real friends are there for you through thick and thin, whether they can be physically there or not. Whether you are on top of the mountain or down in the ditch, they are there. Real friends are there for one another and have one another's backs. The people with whom you spend time are going to make or break your dreams. Not everybody deserves to be around you. You have to defend your light with your life and

Learn who your real friends are.

#68
BE SUPER DISCIPLINED
AND DEDICATED

Discipline is doing what you hate to do,
but doing it like you love it.
— Mike Tyson

In order to accomplish anything, discipline and dedication are required. The greater the accomplishments we go after are, the greater the discipline and dedication required will be. If we want to accomplish greater things, win, and finish on top, then we need to be *super* disciplined and dedicated. There is no room for slacking. There are *no days off.* There is a saying in fighting that says, "When you are not training, someone else is training to kick your ass," which is true, especially when you are competing with the best.

If we want to be the best and compete with the best, we must always be training, learning, and working on our crafts, just like boxers do. And like boxers, we must be consistently consistent. We need to do all we need to do, whatever it takes, to get to where we want to be and act accordingly. We must do all we said we were going to do, whether we want to or not, when the time comes to do it. We must work the muscle of not wanting to do it and then doing it anyway, with as little lag time as possible.

Discipline weighs ounces; regret weighs tons. A sign up on one of the high beams in my gym reads, "Do today what others won't, so tomorrow you can do what others can't."

Be super disciplined and dedicated.

#69
WHEN PEOPLE TELL YOU THAT YOU CAN'T DO IT, PROVE THEM WRONG

Thank you to every person who has told me I can't. You are just another reason I will.
— Manny Paquiao

When someone tells you that you cannot do something, prove them wrong and do it. You can do anything you set your mind to accomplishing. Believe in yourself and never give up.

Do not do something *in order to* prove them wrong *and* prove them wrong. Let it give you extra ammunition, and light a fire under your butt. I have had many encounters with doctors in which they told me I needed knee replacement surgery, an immediate epidural, spinal fusion surgery, a month of anti-inflammatories to make swelling go down, "the purple pill" for six weeks, and much more. I followed none of their advice, and I always proved them wrong. For sure there are occasions where medicine is needed and it is very helpful, but for sure pharmaceuticals are dispensed exponentially more than necessary for the advantage of the pharmaceutical companies and its shareholders, rather than the patient needing the healing. Since my mid-twenties, I have always found a way to heal at the source that caused the issue in the first place and to heal naturally, without pharmaceuticals. I got clear that everything we need exists already inside of us; we just need to access it. When physicians told me I must do things a certain way or take specific medicines, I sought alternative ways and proved them wrong. Like Muhammad Ali said, "Impossible is nothing."

When someone says you cannot do something, say, "*Yet.*" Find someone who has accomplished what you want, in the ways that you want, and follow them. Build a team of advisers who you want advising you. When I made the decision to heal my back without surgery or pharmaceuticals, I took surgeons and medical doctors off my team, as surgeons perform surgery and doctors prescribe medications. I built a team of advisers from whom I wanted advice and who had accomplished things I wanted to accomplish in ways I wanted to accomplish them. For this situation of healing and transformation, I hired an osteopath, a pelvic floor specialist, and a master Pilates instructor. I also got two Pilates Reformer certifications, a breath work coaching certification, and lots of acupuncture, and I did several hundred hours of meditation and a whole lot of following and studying under Dr. Joe Dispenza. He healed his back with his mind, and a lot more than that, yet without the insisted-upon Harrington rod spinal surgery, so I knew I wanted to follow in his footsteps. I did his Advanced Weeklong Meditation Immersion and then his Advanced Follow-Up Meditation workshop and practiced his intense meditations twice daily, and I still do.

So it may not be easy, and almost never is, yet for sure it is possible. The word *impossible* itself has *I'm possible* in it. Knowing it exists, had existed, or could exist, or that we could bring it into existence, we just have to make it happen, in the way we want, and believe, and do what most aligns with our highest and truest selves, no matter what anyone else says or believes. There is a presupposition in neuro-linguistic programming (NLP) that everyone already has all the tools they need to achieve the desired results, as in if someone else can do it, then I can do it too.

Boxers come from adversity. They struggle from the start and live a life of proving, training, planning, and fighting relentlessly to beat the odds. Boxers often do what others have told them they could never do, and most, especially the winners and of course the champions, prove the doubters and naysayers wrong. Like boxers, know that one day the people who never believed in you will talk about how they met you and how you sure did prove them wrong.

When people tell you that you can't do it, prove them wrong.

#70
NEVER GIVE UP

You never lose, till you actually give up.
— Mike Tyson

Push really hard through extreme times and never, ever, ever give up. Quitters never win, so if you want to win, never quit. Have tenacity. Push through the difficult times, and know that no matter what happens, you will be okay and make it through the storm. Know that and say to yourself, "No matter what happens, I got this, and I am not giving up." Make giving up not an option.

Boxers never give up. I have seen hundreds upon hundreds of fights, and I have never seen a boxer just give up. They are there to fight. They do whatever they need to do and whatever it takes as they fight until the end. People are what they will themselves to be, so will yourself to be all you want.

You are here to create your music, not someone else's, so do not die with your music still in you. Keep pushing and striving, be relentless, and

Never give up.

#71
BE IN FLOW

Float like a butterfly, sting like a bee.
— Muhammad Ali

Be in flow. Exist in flow. Movement is medicine. Never stop moving. Boxers have to be light on their feet. Boxers must be like cats, relaxed yet able to pounce at any moment. Boxers need to be in a flow of action and reaction.

When you are in flow in life, work does not feel like work; it feels like play. You become what you resist, so do not resist what you do not want to persist. Be open to anything and attached to nothing. Dance and flow through life.

Everything matters, and then nothing matters. Exist in the space that lies between those two things. All possibilities lie within or between the two polarities. Play in the space. *Be in flow.* It is what it is, and it is about existing in the space between the two opposites. My philosophy of life and fitness is "It's the moments between the notes that create the music; and in sports, it's the moments and spaces between the movements that create the actual music, dance, and flow. Life is a collection of moments; be in the flow of them. It is always about getting to the space in between and playing in the space between the two polarities."

Boxers bob and weave and stick and move in the midst of what is similar to a car crash, and they flow. They have prepared for this and surrendered to this. They become one with the act of doing it.

Things that work are lighter and faster, and things that do not work are darker and heavier. *Be like water. Flow.* Surrender. Be lighter and faster on your feet. Be a boxer in life. Flow so well that you do not get caught, and be ready to knock out whatever is about to smack you before it actually does. Then you can continue to

Be in flow.

#72
LEAVE IT ALL IN THE RING
—GIVE IT YOUR ALL

If I lose I'll walk away and never feel bad because I did all I could.
There was nothing more to do.
— Joe Frazier

You'll never feel the disappointment of "I should have tried harder" if you did the best you could from the start. All you can do is do your best, so make sure you do that, always.

Boxers give it their all, and then they give even more. They push past their perceived limits and leave it all in the ring, with nothing left to spare, especially when it is a toe-to-toe fight until the very end—the fights we all love to watch. When that happens, we watch true warriors in action. It inspires us to do the same. I do not think there are many motivating YouTube videos that do not incorporate boxing, fighting, or working out hard to show grit and pushing past limits. It is what inspires people to take action and give it their all. Seeing others do it can inspire us to do it too, as transformation happens in the sharing.

Do that in life. Just when you think you cannot take anymore, you cannot push any further, or you cannot go on anymore, think of a boxer and know that embodiment can also exist in you. Breathe, channel it, and do all that aligns with giving it your all and never having regrets. When you look back, you will always know you gave it your all and did the absolute best you could. Now, do better. You got this!

Leave it all in the ring and give it your all.

#73
YOU WILL BECOME HUMBLE

If you're not humble, it's going to bring humbleness to you.
— Mike Tyson

For sure, if you stick with the discipline of boxing and allow it to infiltrate and fully affect your life, you will become humble. Boxing humbles you. Romeo, the head boxing trainer at my South Beach Boxing gym, always said, "Boxers are not humble; they're humbled." That is true, as they do not walk in the gym on their first day already humble. Imagine getting beat up and thanking the person who did it for the good job they did. Boxers, through their journey, gain an incredible about of modesty and are humbled. That is one of the greatest beauties of the sport of boxing. It turns boys into men in the army, and it brings humbleness to you. You get knocked down plenty yet get back up more. Life does the same, ideally, if you allow it to, and you learn from your mistakes. You cannot live as if you are better than anyone else because the only person you want to be better than is the person you were yesterday.

Humble people are coachable, at peace with themselves and others, slow to offend, and quick to forgive. They treat everyone with respect, are grateful, listen, speak their minds, put others first, make difficult decisions with ease, and do not think too highly or too lowly of themselves. They are just pleasant, admirable individuals overall. I always say, "I bring out your inner badass, and you become a humble badass." Who does not want to be a humble badass? Arrogance is so ugly and unattractive, and humility is beautiful and strong. Follow the path of the beautiful and strong, and

You will become humble.

#74

BE PRECISE

I'd take precision any day over power.
— Alexis Arguello

Precision beats power. Precision is a must because, if you miss the mark, you miss it in its entirety. Precision is identifying an exact, specific point you want to hit and then hitting it. It is an amazing feeling when it is all you worked for, and it takes a lot of consistent practice to get precise. That is the difference between those at the top and those lower down. Those at the top make their marks and hit their targets bang on, while others miss. Even if they miss only by a smidgen, it is still not precise or on point. The better you get and the more experience you gain, the more precise you get. So much goes into precision—focus, practice, consistency, discipline, patience, and more. You are either right on the mark or not on the mark. Either you hit the target or you do not. Either you are precise or you are not. Either you hit the bull's-eye or you do not. Precision has no gray area; it is exact.

Precision in boxing refers to the timing and accuracy of the punch. Skilled boxers think things through, are strategic, and know exactly where they want to hit their opponents. And they go after it with intentional precision. They focus on being precise and hitting right where they intended to, and then every punch sets up the next. So when they are precise with one punch, it allows them to set themselves up to be precise with the next.

Be precise in life, like boxers in their fights. Focus and know exactly what it is you are going after, and then practice over and over again to be able to perform with precision and constantly hit your targets, bang on. Keep your eyes on the prize and be specific along the way. Being precise gives you confidence that you are doing great and moving in the right direction as you are hitting your targets exactly as you wished, intended, and planned.

Be precise.

#75
EXPERIENCE MOSTLY WINS

With experience in boxing, you learn how to be
a scientific boxer and how to fight easy.
— Manny Paquiao

You don't compare a guy with thirty or forty fights with a guy who
had two hundred fights and fought over twenty-five years.
— Jake Lamotta

I often got upset when older guys would call or come by the gym and say that they wanted to be professional boxers. I felt it was either an obvious lack of knowledge or a disrespect of the sport. I would respond by asking if they thought they could become a Tiger Woods at this point in their careers. For some reason, many people think boxing is just fighting, and if they are good at fighting, they would be great professional boxers. Well, the best fighter is never angry and never fights. Getting to that level, of being calm in the midst of the craziest storm and able to focus, flow, and keep your eyes open in what is equivalent to a consistent car crash, takes many, many years of consistent practice and experience in the ring. Top professional boxers, the champions, are groomed and graduated like prized horses. Boxers who want to win and excel have extremely lengthy amateur careers. Yes, there are always exceptions, but almost all top boxers, especially those below the heavyweights, have well over one hundred amateur fights. Then, once they become professional boxers, they begin with four rounds, graduate to six rounds, then eight rounds, and then ten rounds. And then, if they are deserving enough and great enough, they do twelve rounds, which is a title fight.

Boxers train to thrive and win in a war that is always unpredictable, and they do it daily as their job. So the more they do it, the more they learn. They get better or lose. When a boxer has hundreds of amateur fights under his belt and over twenty professional fights, you know he is experienced. If he fights a new fighter, he will most likely win due to his experience.

It is the same in life. When you want to be successful and thrive, you need to gain the skills and experience. We all know that when we applied for our first jobs, we often heard, "Come back when you have more experience." We have to pay our dues, lay the groundwork, and be consistent. If we want to be known for something and excel at it, we need to work harder than anyone else to stand out from the rest. Gain experience if you like winning, as

Experience mostly wins.

#76
YOU WILL LEARN HOW STRONG YOU REALLY ARE

Impossible is just a big word thrown around by small men who find it easier to live in the world they've been given than to explore the power they have to change it. Impossible is not a fact. It's an opinion. Impossible is not a declaration. It's a dare. Impossible is potential. Impossible is temporary. Impossible is nothing.
— Muhammad Ali

Nothing is impossible; it is just a barrier we create in our minds. Know that if someone has accomplished it, it is not impossible. You need to decide that you want something and that you are going after it, and then make it a "must do," not a "should do." Prove to yourself how strong you really are. Let nothing stop you from attaining and reaching your goal. All it takes is a decision, and then you can figure out the rest along the way. When you push past your limits, fight through the storm, and refuse to give up no matter what, as your goal is more important than any excuses, you get to discover how very strong you really are. How amazing is that? You can't always see it during the fight, but when you are done, when you have gone through the storm and come out on the other end alive and thriving, you realize it was all worth it, as nothing feels better than strength. You will feel like the hero you are.

Just like boxers who are skilled and great at what they do, you can prove to yourself how strong you really are. They fight through wars and come out on top. They become like superheroes when, over and over again, they prove to themselves the extent of their strength. They break records; push past their limits; always surpass their previous accomplishments; and just constantly seek to get smarter, better, greater, faster, and stronger.

If you are not getting stronger, you are getting weaker, as nothing stays the same. You are stronger than you think you are. Prove to yourself in life how strong you really are. Make goals and crush them. Never give up. Impress yourself. Surprise yourself. Decide what it is you are going after and go after it relentlessly. Always seek strength and be strong because it is the best feeling in the world. Nothing is impossible, as impossible is nothing. Know this and

You will learn how strong you really are.

#77
TEMPTATION IS A REAL THING

Temptation is the biggest drug in the world.
— Mike Tyson

Always think before you act, which requires slowing down a bit. Do not be so quick to react and make a choice without thinking of the outcome or consequences. We all have moments when we make commitments while feeling amazing, and then there are moments when we do not want to honor them. We make excuses to get what we want in the moment, and the excuses are so valid to us that we cheat.

Temptation is a real thing. Know what your temptations are and set up systems before those temptation triggers occur. Romeo, the head boxing trainer at my gym, always says, "Be careful, as some choices will send you to the moon." Care is needed because hindsight is a wonderful concept that we do not possess before a choice is made. Make wise choices beforehand, weigh your options, and do not choose to do something you know can possibly send you to the moon.

Boxers live such extreme and intense lives. When they are in training camp, they are focused on only that. Many get into the high life of sex and drugs as a release from living the extreme opposite of total discipline. I have always said that the difference between champion boxers and nonchampion boxers is that the champions stay in shape and always keep fit. It is a lifestyle, not a short-term goal. Some boxers require constant supervision in order to stay strict and on point with all of the training and the extremely focused and disciplined lifestyle it entails.

In life we all have things that tempt us. Know what your temptations are and create boundaries so that they will not trigger you or you will not give in to them. Preplan, and preact, to avoid caving into your temptations, and set yourself up for success, rather than subjecting yourself to temptation. Temptation will only set you back and bring you down if you cave into it. And know that, whenever you are not on the ball, someone else is on the ball planning to surpass you in whatever it is you are striving to reach. Do not give in to your temptations. Know what they are and avoid accordingly, as

Temptation is a real thing.

#78
DON'T SHOW WEAKNESSES

I'm scared every time I go in the ring, but it's how you handle it. What you have to do is plant your feet, bite down on your mouthpiece and say, "Let's go."
— Mike Tyson

We all have strengths, and we all have weaknesses. We want to focus on our strengths and sharpen our best tools. We do not want to ignore our weaknesses, yet we also do not want to brag about or expose them either. Boxers have styles that make all the fights different and exciting, and fighters come out showing their strengths, not exploiting their weaknesses. If they did show their weaknesses, their opponents would not have anything to figure out and would know exactly what to do to win. Boxers will fight to their strengths and not show their weaknesses.

It's the same in life. You want to work on your strengths and show all your best to the world. Why point out what is not good when you can show what is good? Be strong and do what strong does. Practice what you need to, whatever you are weak in, but do not exploit yourself by showing what you are not good at, as people will remember what you show them.

Don't show weaknesses.

#79
PAIN AND SUFFERING
ARE PART OF IT

I hated every minute of training but I said, Don't quit.
Suffer now and live the rest of your life as a champion.
— Muhammad Ali

We live in a world of polarity. You would not have joy if you did not have pain. Pain is just a speed bump to success. It is part of the process, so work on getting used to it and not freaking out when you encounter it, as it is to be expected. We sell shirts at my gym that say, "Pain is weakness leaving the body." Just let it go. Flow through it. That which we resist persists, so just breathe through it and know it is all temporary.

Boxers are always confronted with pain. Boxers are in the hitting business. They flow and fight through pain. They train for it, with it, and through it. It's amazing, yet with practice, you can get better at anything. And if pain is part of the process and a part of life, you are better off knowing how to cope and deal with it. Otherwise, it prolongs and bleeds into other areas of your life and makes you miserable. Use pain as a teacher rather than medicating or hiding from it. Acceptance and acknowledgment are the way. Notice it, breathe through it, and then have a plan of action to get through it effectively to its other side, which is joy.

Whatever is holding you back from your peace, make the peace. Whatever has happened to you has also happened for you. The only way out is in; therefore, you need to go through the pain to get out of it. There is no going around it. Ask yourself if you are going through it or growing through it, as you want to do both. And know that

Pain and suffering are part of it.

#80
HOW YOU TRAIN IS
HOW YOU FIGHT

If you work hard in training, the fight is easy.
— Manny Paquiao

It's less about the physical training in the end, than it is about the mental preparation: boxing is a chess game. You have to be skilled enough, and have trained hard enough to know how many different ways you can counterattack in any situation, at any moment.
— Jimmy Smits

For the most part, how we do one thing is how we do everything. We need to build the habits that are necessary for what we want to create for ourselves and our lives. We must cultivate our desired behaviors that produce our desired outcomes. We cannot expect to win if we do not practice, study, and train to win.

Notice whether there is something in your life you are wanting to win at and are having to fight for, and then make sure that you are doing all it takes for the outcome you want to come to fruition. There is always a recipe to follow, as success leaves clues, and then you can add your own flair and make it even greater. Remember that sign in my gym: "Do today what others won't, so tomorrow you can do what others can't." You choose the way, and there is always a way.

It is the habits and ways of being that create champions. Boxers would not even think to do less than all it takes in their training and preparation for their fights to win. Boxers are clear that how they train is how they fight. Optimal training is needed to win, yet just because fighters' training is on point in all areas does not ensure that they will win. Yet if boxers did not train intelligently and hard, they would not win. It is not luck that gets the boxers their wins. It is their lifestyle, training, and consistent habits and disciplines.

As you can see from all these rules, great boxers are total badasses. They envision their wins and train accordingly. They know by the results of their fights if they have trained hard enough. Nobody trains to lose. Train lazy; fight lazy. Train smart and hard; fight smart and hard.

Know what you want and what it takes to get it. How you prepare will always translate to your performance. Champions are made when nobody is watching. Train in life for whatever it is you are wanting to go after and achieve. You reap what you sow.

How you train is how you fight.

#81
DON'T TAKE UNNECESSARY PUNISHMENT

I took unnecessary punishment when I was fighting,
Subconsciously—I didn't know it then—I
fought like I didn't deserve to live."
— Jake La Motta

Like Kenny Rogers sang in his song "The Gambler," "You got to know when to hold 'em, know when to fold 'em, know when to walk away, know when to run." Some boxers really love the fight and take unnecessary punishment despite being instructed by their corners to make different moves or get out of the corner and never take unnecessary punishment. They are already in a fight and get hit enough—why take extra hits?

When you know that something, someone, or somewhere can get you in trouble, avoid it as best as you can. When you do get into trouble, know how to get out if it, or at least to not get into more of it and make things even worse. Just because you can handle it does not mean you should take it, especially unnecessarily. Become aware. Notice. Plan ahead. Avoid that which does not serve you as best as possible. Know that you *deserve* to live a created life you love and don't take anything less than that which does not align. Have boundaries, as shit happens, but take charge and

Don't take unnecessary punishment.

#82
ROLL WITH THE PUNCHES

That's my gift. I let the negativity roll of me like water
off a duck's back. If it's not positive, I didn't hear it.
If you can overcome that, fights are easy.
— George Foreman

Sometimes you just have to roll with the punches. Boxers learn early on to anticipate incoming punches. Instead of bracing for impact, they move with it to lessen the force. In turn, they also then hit back with the power generated from the punch they just received. So they take it and then give it back to an even greater degree.

In life, you also want to be able to take what comes your way, avoid absorbing it, and then give it back even greater. You want to be able to cope with challenges, withstand adversity, and let the wind help carry you. Do not go against it and get rocked by it. Where we resist, things persist. Do not allow difficulties or criticism to affect you. Do not make things heavy and significant. Disassociate to separate yourself from what is happening. Take a step back and roll with it. Know that in the spectrum of life, it does not really matter and *this too shall pass*. Know you can get through anything; just make sure to go with the flow and

Roll with the punches.

#83
FIGHT WHEN YOU DON'T WANT TO FIGHT

Don't quit. Suffer now and live the rest of your life as a champion.
— Muhammad Ali

Delay gratification, stick it out, and go after what you really want without hesitation or submitting to feelings that could pull you away from achieving it. You will have all you worked for and wanted, and it will all be worth it. You just have to go after it and fight for it, even when you do not feel like it. Boxers cannot procrastinate. That is not a choice they give themselves. Not wanting to fight is not an option, so fighters keep fighting whether they want to or not. As Sly Stallone's character says in *Rocky IV*, "Going in one more round when you don't think you can—that's what makes all the difference in your life." Even if you think you cannot keep going, get ready to surprise yourself and show what you really can accomplish when you do keep going and do not give up. We all already know what giving up feels like, and it is not rewarding. So suffer in the moment, yet reap the benefits for the longer term.

In life, when you are fighting for something worthwhile and have been going after it, keep fighting and pushing through whether you want to or not. You are probably not going to want to, as it is hard work and a struggle to put up a fight, but when all is said and done, you want to know that you did all you set out to do and accomplish regardless of how you felt about it. It is not about your feelings; it is about your commitments and what you planned and set out to do. Do not stop and quit. Keep fighting, and

Fight when you don't want to fight.

#84
COME OUT WINNING

Boxers have to have the skill, and the will, but
the will must be stronger than the skill.
— Muhammad Ali

If you do not begin with a winning mindset and as a winner, you will not end up as a winner. Richard Bandler, best known for being the cocreator of neuro-linguistic programming and from whom I received my master practitioner license in NLP, says, "The one who licks his lips before he fights will be the winner." He means that the one who can taste it will win it. These boxers come out with a winning posture, energy, and entrance and act as if they have already won the fight before it even begins. Boxers must come out and enter the ring as a winner. So much of the fight is won before the fighters even step into the ring. Mindset has everything to do with the way the fight goes and the outcome.

In life, if you begin a winner and have a winning mindset, you are already halfway there. Think, be, and act as if you have already won, and live accordingly to achieve it. Plan to win, think you are going to win, see the win, do what it takes to win, taste the win, behave as the winner, and

Come out winning.

#85
DON'T UNDERESTIMATE YOUR OPPONENTS, AND DON'T OVERESTIMATE THEM EITHER

If you ever dream of beating me you'd better wake up and apologize.
— Muhammad Ali

Assumption is the mother of the screw-up.
— Angelo Dundee

Do not make assumptions. Do your homework. Do not guess. Learn and be in the know. If boxers underestimate their opponents, they will have a real tough job defending themselves in the ring and probably will not win, as they assumed their opponents were worse than they really are. If boxers overestimate their opponents, they carry unnecessary fear and worry because their opponents are not even as great as assumed.

In life, the less you guesstimate, approximate, and assume, the better off you will be. You will have fewer mistakes and more accuracy. It is important to do your due diligence and your homework so you always know what you are up against and can plan and prepare accordingly. The less you leave up to approximation, the closer you will be to the desired target. When dealing with people, including adversaries, in life and in business, deal with them at face value. Ask lots of questions, get clear wherever you are not, deal with the facts you have, and do not make assumptions.

Don't underestimate your opponents, and don't overestimate them either.

#86
STAY ACTIVE,
KEEP MOVING, NEVER STOP

All fighters run. The constant motion prepares you for
being in the ring. And running strengthens your legs.
Punching power comes from your lower body.
— Laila Ali

Think about how boxers do not stay in one spot for more than two seconds. They are always moving. It is super difficult to hit a moving target. Boxers need to always keep moving so they are more difficult to hit. The goal of boxers is to hit and not get hit, so they need to hit and get moving. Get the job done and get out quick.

In life, you want to stay in action, as learning what you do not want to do is just as valuable as learning what you do want. Opportunities do not just knock on your door. You want to pursue what you are after, and if something better comes along, you can pivot and shift accordingly.

Also, the fastest way to change your state of being is to move your body. Movement is medicine, and motion is like lotion for the body. Stay in motion. Things in motion stay in motion, so get moving and build momentum. We need to retrain our bodies to be in a peak state because when we are, we can then have a peak performance and produce optimal results.

Stay active, keep moving, never stop.

#87
STUDY YOUR COMPETITION, OUTWIT YOUR OPPONENTS, AND CREATE LEVERAGE

If a guy beats me once, he'll have to do it again to make me believe him.
— Sugar Ray Leonard

Study your opponents' assets and their flaws. Boxers look for ways to outwit their opponents. It is like a chess game, and each player wants to throw the other off their game, take control, and win. The key is to encourage your opponent to make mistakes so you can capitalize on them. People think you can get in the ring and see the red mist, but it is not about aggression. It is about avoiding being knocked out.

In life, find where you have an advantage, and know that an advantage is only an advantage if you use it. Be a product of self-education. Study. Do things nobody else does, and do them better.

Study your competition, outwit your opponents, and create leverage.

#88
BE PROUD OF YOURSELF—
CELEBRATE YOUR WINS

I'm a winner each and every time I go into the ring.
— George Foreman

Celebrate progress, rather than give excuses. Get used to that. Take it one little step at a time, and it will infiltrate your life. Celebrate when you accomplish things big or small. Get good at cheering for yourself, and have a volume control for the voices in your head. Mute the voices that disempower you, and raise the volume on those that inspire you.

Boxers for sure celebrate their wins. They all have celebrations and after-parties. When boxers win, they are very clear that their hard work paid off, and they are proud of themselves. When boxers hear the announcer say, "And the new" or "And still," it is the greatest feeling in the world. They are the winners, and they feel it and celebrate it.

Rest when your commitments are fulfilled. Take time to relax and recharge in nature so you do not burn out.

Be proud of yourself and celebrate your wins.

#89
INSPIRE OTHERS TO BE GREAT
—SERVE

*Success is attaining your dream while helping others
to benefit from that dream materializing.*
— Sugar Ray Leonard

Service to others is the rent you pay for a room here on Earth.
— Muhammad Ali

The secret to living is giving. When you give, you can authentically be happy and fulfilled as service to others equals joy for yourself. When you seek happiness for yourself, it will always elude you; and when you seek happiness for others, you will always find it. In order to receive we must give. Receiving is reserved for those who give. Giving is what starts the receiving process; therefore, it is better to give than receive.

Find a way to serve and live with a service mentality. Serve as an extension of *who you are in this world*. Your expressions out in the world are *you*. Teach and share your visions and contribute to others as it is service to many that leads to greatness. If you help enough people get what they want, you can have everything you want.

I always say, "It's better to be interested than interesting." Truly listen to others and be present, as it is the best gift you can give. Be a blessing in the lives of everyone you encounter. If you ever want to cheer yourself up, go out and cheer up somebody else. Always think ahead, and if there is something else you could do or say to make it easier for the next person, then do or say just that. Follow the Golden Rule, "Do onto others, as you would have them done unto you." That has always been my religion. Angelo Dundee said, "It don't cost nothing to be nice," and I say, "Serve and get joy in return, as it actually costs a lot to *not* be nice."

If you do not have a vision that serves others, your vision is too small. It is your passion for your vision that keeps you motivated and on your toes. You can then hold yourself accountable more easily to practice what you preach and walk your talk as it inspires you. As a result, you inspire others to be great because transformation happens in the sharing.

Boxers love to serve and give back as they appreciate all the guidance and support they got along the way themselves. Boxers know that they would never be where they got to be without the support they had from their coaches, mentors, trainers, and others who helped them along the way. They like to give back in the same way, and they know the immense need for our youth and our future, and they know the value boxing brings to people's lives.

Use your life as a vehicle to serve. I like to call it "*business in balance.*" *Serve and contribute* as an extension of who you are *and* what you do, in all the roles you play. The secret to living is giving. I have a sign in my kitchen that says,

> Do all the good you can
> In all the ways you can
> At all the places you can
> To all the people you can
> As long as ever you can
> (Shrii Shrii Anandamurti)

My Prayer: Ask and You Shall Receive

God, *use me!* Show me how I will be of best use serving. Show me how I will

Inspire others to be great and serve.

#90
HIRE AND HAVE A COACH

Don't be afraid to employ people that will
force you out of your comfort zone.
— George Foreman

Boxing is a science. You do not just walk into a boxing gym, start punching the heavy bags, and then one day become a great boxer. All fighters have different physical abilities and skills, and that is the coach's influence at work.

People can do more than they ever believed they could do physically, emotionally, mentally, and academically when they have a coach. You have to be pushed, encouraged, developed, guided, and held accountable. Every coach needs a coach, as nobody can see what is in their own blind spots. It is the same with Alcoholics Anonymous and its sponsors. We all need a sponsor, a committed listener, a coach.

Hire mentors. Know that you are always learning, so respect people who have accomplished more than you have. Hire them to guide and coach you to your next level. You do not know what you do not know, and remember, while you are not training, someone else is training to kick your ass. You want to be able to be the best you can be, and that requires a coach or mentor—someone who will see what you do not see and who will tell you what you need to know. Build your team of advisers *and* your go-to's.

Hire the best to be the best. You definitely want a mentor, trainer, coach, or someone who can see things that you do not see and is looking out for your best interests. Stop battling yourself, and when you do go to battle, you are more likely to succeed and win if you find a mentor or

Hire and have a coach.

#91
SOMETIMES THE TOWEL
NEEDS TO BE THROWN IN

We all think we've got one more boxing match in us, and that, probably will be the downfall of Floyd Mayweather, George Foreman, Manny Paquiao. We'll overstay our welcome.
— George Foreman

Fighters never throw in the towel, as they are the fighters, and deciding when to end a fight is a reason they have coaches. Fighters never give up and never quit, which is another reason their corners are so important. The people in the corner ensure their fighters stay safe and alive and do not take unnecessary punishment. If the corner feels a fighter is for sure losing a fight, taking too much punishment, and losing every round, they may decide to throw in the towel and end the fight before risking too much damage to their fighter. It does not happen often, yet it is an option and a safety measure.

In life, you may also need to throw in the towel at times. You want to cut your losses before they become too catastrophic and unrepairable. Know when you are fighting a losing battle and get out while you still can. Fight battles worth fighting for. Sometimes it is more beneficial to quit what is not going to work out than to carry on and get pummeled. Know the difference, as

Sometimes the towel needs to be thrown in.

#92
EVERY PUNCH SETS UP THE NEXT
—GENERATE POWER

*It's like someone jammed an electric light bulb in your face, and
busted it. I thought half my head was blowed off.... When he
knocked me down I could have stayed there for three weeks.*
— James J. Braddock

Everything you do has an effect on everything else. If you do not do something well, then the next item in the order will not be good either. In boxing, the jab is a boxer's most important punch as it is their lead punch and the one that sets up the rest of the punches. If one punch is not good, then the next one is not good either. The jab measures and gauges, and once boxers see an opening or a way to create one, they then set up the rest of their punches and combinations in such a way that they generate power. They use every punch to pick up power from the previous punch. Boxers do not throw one punch; they throw punches in bunches, as that is how they generate power.

In life, build momentum, generate power, and set things up to stack on previous items, making it all that much better. Know that everything you do matters and has an effect on everything else that comes after it. You are only as strong as your weakest link. Know that

Every punch sets up the next and generate power.

#93
CONTROL YOUR BREATHING: SELF-REGULATE

You know if you want to be a boxer the first time
you get hit on the nose.
— Ricky Hatton

All professional sports differ in the way the athletes breathe. If you can get the breathing down, you will be much better at the sport. You will become one with the activity you are doing, your breath will keep you in the present moment, and you will be most effective. Our breath is what keeps us alive. We came into this world with a first breath, and we will leave this world with a final, last breath. When I was talking to Mike Tyson about the importance of breathing and breath work, he told me he did not even realize it or focus on his breath, as he just is who he is authentically, according to him, "a sophisticated savage." He expressed that he is not an athlete but a true fighter 'til the end, the best ever. It was not a practice for him; it was just how he breathes. I guess it is like telling a lion what ferocious is; he just *is*. Tyson took a deep breath for me to show me how he breathes, and I thought I was in the room with a dragon. The expansion capacity he has in his lungs and chest is mind blowing. And here I am, having earned my breath coaching certification and practicing breath and different breathing patterns several times daily, and it is challenging for me. But Tyson just does it like a superhuman. I will never forget the image of him taking in all that oxygen—truly inspiring. When I meditate and do breath work, I visualize Mike Tyson sucking up air like the most powerful vacuum ever, and it truly helps me go deeper in my own breathing practice. The more oxygen you take in and the deeper and fuller you breathe, the better. Breathe as if you have a large nose on your chest and heart, and inhale through your heart center, fully and deeply.

Humans are the only species that can self-regulate. We do this through our breath. How you breathe is everything. Breath is the fuel of the body. Breathing is done consciously and voluntarily or unconsciously and involuntarily. The goal is to breathe deeply, slowly, quietly, and more regularly, as that is when you are in harmony. When your breath is rapid, shallow, irregular, and abnormal, you are then breathing in states of upset and anger, and your heart and brain are not in coherence. Your thinking, and then your feelings, determine your breathing. Pay attention to your regular breath without doing a thing and just notice it. When there is negativity, *stack good moments*, breathe deep, *feel* strong, and think of a moment in your life when you felt deeply grateful. Breathe and step into the moment as if you are there *now* and self-regulate. When you hold your breath, you always have fear and anxiety. Breathe deeply, slowly, fully, to the east, and to the west through your whole chest cavity and let it expand and contract fully.

When breathing, do more east-to-west breathing rather than north-and-south. The more east-and-west, 360-degree breathing you have, the healthier you are. When talking, make sure to exhale with your speaking and then inhale in the spaces between words. Ask someone to tell you if your mouth is open while you're sleeping, and work on consciously sleeping with your mouth closed. Become a nose breather if you are not. Breathing through your nose can help filter out dust and allergens, humidify the air you breathe, and boost your oxygen intake. Nasal breathing produces nitric oxide, cleans the air as it enters the body, and does the same amount of work with less energy expended. Work on breathing only in and out of your nose except when working out or exerting a lot of energy that then requires you to open your mouth. In a boxing match, boxers can choose to take a knee, which is like a standing eight count but at the fighter's discretion. Boxers do not often do this, but sometimes it can save them in the fight because they can regain their breath, get eight seconds to self-regulate, and get back in the fight. They will lose a point, but it may be worth it as it is a last resort for the fighter and a decision they must make to be able to continue on fighting.

Control your breathing. Self-regulate.

JOLIE
GLASSMAN

#94
ALWAYS BE IN SHAPE AND
SUPER FIT AND LEAN

I run, but boxing conditioning is different, so you have to get used to running in the ring. Boxing movements are very different. I train very hard at things that mimic boxing. I have to do mostly sport-specific training, such as lots of sparring.
— Wladimir Klitschko

Generally, the more weight you put on, the less effective you are.
— Sugar Ray Leonard

I have always adhered to two principles. The first one is to train hard and get in the best physical condition. The second is to forget about the other fellow until you face him in the ring and the bell sounds for the fight.
— Rocky Marciano

Boxers at the top of their game, and those truly seeking to become champions, are always in shape. They fight often and always need to meet the weight requirements. Boxers get fined substantially and possibly get disqualified if they do not make weight. It is very difficult if their weight fluctuates, which is why they do not veer too far away from their weight class and work to stay fit, lean, and in shape. Boxers are always training and working on getting better, fitter, stronger, faster, and more skilled, which is the same concept and theme of my gym. Mike Tyson told me that he does what he knows nobody else will do, such as waking up at two in the morning to go running in the snow, so he can win before he even enters the ring. He is always in shape, fit, and determined, as a champion needs to be.

Stay in shape so you do not have to keep getting into shape. When you start taking care of yourself, you start feeling better, you start looking better, and you start to attract better. It all starts within you. Prevention is easier than correction. Make being fit a *must*, not a *should*, and you will always be fit and in shape. Work out consistently and always. It is a daily habit, like brushing your teeth, that must be honored to stay in shape. Fitness is not for an occasion; it is for life, and it is to be done daily as a practice to

Always be in shape and be super fit and lean.

#95
THERE ARE NO SHORTCUTS
TO SUCCESS

I've found that taking shortcuts will get you to the place you don't want to be much quicker than they get you to the place you want to be.
— Lennox Lewis

Life is a journey. Take it step by step. It is a process, so enjoy it. There are no shortcuts to success, and there are no secrets to it, as it is all in a book somewhere. Most boxers, aside from a few record breakers, began boxing very young, and those who became champions know what it took to get there. Boxers fight their way to the top, literally, and the good ones, the well-taken-care-of ones, are groomed strategically like prized horses.

Boxers pay their dues. So many ingredients, as you have read in this book, go into the making of a champion boxer. There are no shortcuts to get there. Those who are at the top struggled and fought their way there, one step at a time, just like all the others.

Know that, in life, there are no shortcuts to success. You have to follow the rules in this book like they are the law, as they are if you want to be ultra-successful and stay that way. Just accept that it will be a lot of work, and a lot of hard work, yet it will all be worth it when you give it your all and you live life as the journey it is, knowing there are no shortcuts to living your best life.

There are no shortcuts to success.

#96
RECOVERY IS A DAILY MUST

An injury is not just a process of recovery, it is also a process of discovery.
— Conor McGregor

I always say, "The moments between the notes create the music." The in-between is very important and needed for the process and the whole. What we surrender to, we allow. We must create space in the body. We must recover and heal daily, and all of that occurs only during rest. We must learn to relax, chill out, and be in our parasympathetic, autonomic nervous systems of rest and digest so we are not operating under the hormones of stress, as healing and recovery in the sympathetic system cannot occur when we do. Also daily, we need active recovery, such as stretching, focused breath work, foam rolling, trigger-point therapy, myofascial release, and so on. Make sure to have a kickass morning routine that inspires you and centers you for the day ahead that begins with meditation, a practice of gratitude, warm lemon water, stretching, and prepping your food if you have not already. Then have a kickass turn-down, nighttime routine that prepares you for a great night's rest. Eat like you love yourself. Move like you love yourself. Speak like you love yourself. Act like you love yourself. Recover like you love yourself. Just love yourself. Know that self-care is your superpower, so exercise it.

Boxers and professional athletes know the importance of recovery. They have teams of professionals who work with them to optimize their recovery so they can optimize their athleticism. Recovery is often active. Sometimes it is rest, and sometimes it is active. I always say there is a fine line between recovering and getting out of shape. Do not allow the latter. The better we recover, the stronger we will be and the better we can perform. Your best, greatest, and *free* coach is *your body*. Learn to really listen to your body and act accordingly.

Recovery is a daily must.

#97
HEALTH AND DIET ARE
OF TOP PRIORITY

You have to fight for your health and stay on top of it.
Our bodies are meant to be healthy.
— Laila Ali

Will Smith once told me, while he was training at my gym for his lead role as Muhammad Ali in the *Ali* movie, "The keys to life are running and reading—reading to learn all you want because knowledge is power and running to beat that voice in your head." Challenging yourself and always pushing yourself past your limits is where you will grow, be productive, and succeed. How you do one thing is how you do everything, for the most part, and that behavior carries over to all other areas of your life. *Health is wealth.* Learn all you can, seek different opinions, and know that ultimately you are in charge. Stay the course, beat that voice in your head, flourish, and only do things that have you continue in that desirable direction.

When I was a young kid, around the age of thirteen years old, my skin would break out, and it was embarrassing, as were many things in becoming a teenager. My mom would take me to the dermatologist for a brief appointment in which they would have me spend more time updating records and filling out paperwork than addressing the issue. I would leave with hundreds of pills of the antibiotic tetracycline. I remember they would have it there in stock—and boy, did they have stock in this *medicine*. The office lady opened a closet door filled with the pills from top to bottom and literally asked me the quantity I wanted. I could get a hundred pills for ten dollars, and I was recommended to take them daily and always. How insane was that? I would walk out with arms full of antibiotics. After all, it was going to clear up my skin. Well, it never really did. I went through stages of broken-out skin and the journey of getting to the bottom of such changes. The recommended antibiotics to clear up my skin then messed up my gut in my future, made me less resistant to antibiotics working in my future, and who knows what else.

Then, when I was seventeen years old, I went to my gynecologist for a routine visit. I had severe menstrual cramps, and I was prescribed birth control to help with cramps and irregularity in my menstrual cycle. At that time, I was also prescribed Paxil, an antidepressant, for my moodiness that occurred a few days before my periods. I was just a teenager trying to utilize coping skills I had been taught and that had been instilled in me. Did I really need to be medicated?

227

Well, once I met my ex-husband in my early twenties, he learned I was taking these medications and was shocked. He was British, and that was not happening in England. Where he came from, they dealt with things and worked through them, without medications. So I listened and agreed, and I stopped taking these two medications. Wow, was that difficult. So began my health journey, branching out into whole-life health. I got clear that life was about health span, not life span. I was already working out like crazy, trying to get strong and fit and look good, and then I was not feeling good in many areas. And these medications I was being prescribed did not get rid of what was going on in the first place. Going off birth control caused me to gain lots of weight and experience mood swings, and my face developed tons of brown markings called melasma, the effects of which lasted for a long time. I did not feel right, in many ways, and I knew that I was never going back on something like that again in my future. Then I began weaning off the Paxil. I swear I had suicidal thoughts during that process, even though I was always, for the most part, a happy, confident person. It was all because of withdrawing from these medications.

At the time, medications were not advertised on television just yet, but for sure doctors were getting kickbacks for publicly traded drugs that they were dispensing at large. I remember calling my ex-husband and feeling brave enough to tell him I was scared and having rampant suicidal thoughts. He told me to call the doctor immediately. I did, and they said to wean off more slowly, so I did. These Paxil pills were super tiny to begin with, and I was having to wean off in quarters, taking what was equivalent in size to a crumb to be able to get off it. I was finally able to rid myself of medications.

Well, here came my wake-up call in my health journey. I was a schoolteacher at the time and was always teaching and speaking to large classrooms of people. My voice was always hoarse, and I often had a sore throat and got sick. I believed it was because I was an elementary schoolteacher, and all the kids were always sick and spreading germs. Well, whenever I got sick, my throat was the first thing to close off and shut down fully due to it being so swollen. So I went to an ear, nose, and throat (ENT) doctor, and he did not even look at me or ask me anything. He just said, "Take Nexium, the 'purple pill,' for six weeks to two months and then come back and see me. You have acid reflux." Well, that was the final straw for me. I went home so upset and said, "I'm not taking this purple pill. He didn't even diagnose me!" I stayed awake through the night researching acid reflux, where it comes from, and how to cure it naturally, without medications. I was done with turning to doctors for all ailments. In a world of information, ignorance is a choice, and I no longer wanted to be ignorant. I found lots of information, and what first worked was a mini shot of apple cider vinegar in the morning and before bedtime. And when I felt this acid reflux coming on, I would have a slice of an apple and a teaspoon of honey. Well, I never went back to the doctor, and that bout or episode ended and I was fine. It must have worked.

I am a believer in a whole-language, whole-life approach. You need to read it, live it, see it, believe it, talk about it, be about it, learn about it, and immerse yourself in it fully. It becomes a lifestyle. You are what you eat. We have all heard that before, and it is so commonly said and known for no other reason than it is true. Everything you do and eat contributes to the person you are becoming. The meat and dairy industries are the biggest businesses and causes of our pollution, the destruction of our planet, and the decline in our physical and mental health. What the United States allows for our nutrition—what they condone, encourage, and profit from—is disheartening and disgraceful.

So on I went, continuing my journey of health and wellness. I read a book back in 2004 called *Natural Cures They Don't Want You to Know About* by Kevin Trudeau, and it forever changed my life. Now, I have always been into fitness and stayed away from junk food, yet knowledge is power. How healthy did I want to be? Well, I did not want to be at the mercy of doctors and their dispensaries. This book had me change so many habits and things in my life. It really opened my eyes. I stopped using a microwave, I got a water filtration system on my entire house, and I stopped eating publicly traded, big-name brand, packaged foods. And I certainly was not going to take any medications. I became way more aware and conscious. I highly recommend reading the book. Even though I read it back in 2004, it is still amazing and will change your life. It's crazy how the food *and* drug industry is one business, together. I always say it would be best if food and drugs were not able to be publicly traded on the stock market and were not together as one business. The primary goal for publicly traded companies is to keep the profits high and the costs low, no matter what. They make the food addicting, and to fix that, you will need the drugs. If you go to a local drugstore, the medicines at the front counters are common treatments for what people are currently suffering from, such as, acid reflux and heartburn. Now allergy medications are everywhere. These products and companies put so much garbage, crap, fillers, and chemicals in our diets, and it is supposed to nourish us.

Now everyone is different, and we all have different make-ups. As I mention in the "Hire a Coach" chapter, your best coach is *your own body! Learn to listen to it.* Immerse yourself in a life of health, fitness, wellness, good nutrition, balance, strength, and flexibility and in a journey to always becoming the greater, and greatest, version of yourself. Life is a journey, and you will take it as it comes; yet the more prepared and knowledgeable you are when things do come your way, the more intelligently you can react. Prevention is much easier than correction. Know that you have a full pharmacy within you that you just need to access to heal. Everything you need already exists inside of you; just get quiet enough to listen and do not pollute your body so you can be most clear, balanced, and healthy.

No matter what has come my way since my late twenties and my many previous run-ins with the medical field, including being prescribed medications throughout my later teenage years unnecessarily, I have always sought out a team of people to help me on my journey to recovery without surgery or pharmaceuticals. It's funny how people always say, "Get a second opinion," and I always think or say, "I get several, and then I decide what resonates best with me." Resonate, based on kinesiology, because your own individual body knows best. *We know*, as we are crossing through things, what feels right or good and what does not. I always seek natural ways and alternatives toward healing and recovery. It is for sure not an easy route, yet it does not have side effects. It utilizes what I am able to do on my own, with extensive research and practices to get strong and healthy again. To solve a problem or issue, you need to remove the cause, not the symptom, and most medical doctors treat symptoms.

Back in 2011, I was in a motorcycle accident, and I got thrown to the other side of the street. I had no helmet on my head. My ex-boyfriend and I were riding home from dinner one evening near my home, and a taxicab turned into us. I was taken to the hospital in an ambulance, and I had to get my head stapled up, as it was split open. I ended up having eleven herniated discs, vertigo, and a concussion that lasted almost six months. During my healing and recovery time, I got into another mini car accident when a senior citizen rolled his car backward right into mine while we were waiting on an incline to get into a parking garage. And that little accident made everything way, way worse. I was not in a position to handle another major jolt. That's when my journey to seek and learn and to heal and recover naturally began. I got into physical therapy and variations of recovery, and I did Pilates daily. I then got two Pilates certifications as well. I learned so much. I healed to the point that I was able to train again, as all that mattered to me was being able to box. I was not able to kickbox much anymore, yet I was able to box, thank God. I read a bunch of books, such as *Treat Your Own Back*, *Treat Your Own Neck*, *Treat Your Own Knees*, all by Robin Mackenzie, and I read *The Supple Leopard* and several other anatomy and recovery books.

Then, eight years later, in 2019, my lower back acted up again, and I had a major episode. I could not walk or get out of bed. Boy, was this one hell of a scare. I first tried to heal things on my own with rest, ice, and acupuncture, but nothing was working. So I got an MRI on just my lower back, as I wanted to deal with this major episode. I went to two different orthopedic surgeons, and they both told me I needed an epidural and immediate fusion surgery. I share this because, when building your team, make sure all members align. And if you want to go the natural route and not undergo surgery, then do not have a surgeon as one of your advisers. I remember I cried in my office as I thought about how in the world I was going to get up the stairs to my gym while recovering from fusion surgery.

I decided I was not going the surgery route. First, I tried decompression, and maybe that could have helped, but learning to relax and chill out was a major part of my recovery for this, and having to go there five days a week, adding almost twenty hours to my already hectic schedule, was not conducive to relaxing. So I went to an osteopath, who felt I should not do decompression because he was concerned that I would compress even more when walking around again after repetitive decompression treatments. He wanted me to do these specific strengthening exercises daily in my home, specific swimming exercises daily, continue with my acupuncture, and do Pilates. Well, I was in a bind as I did not want to continue to do two opposing things. So since I was not able to relax, I was not doing anything to assist in my recovery while going to decompression, and the lack of movement was also driving me bonkers, I decided to quit the decompression and follow only this osteopath's advice. Immediately, that very next day, it is like the gates of surety opened for me. I knew that if I followed protocol and did all he said, I was on the way to recovery and would be back to my boxing training in time, not on the journey to spinal fusion surgery. He was right, and it was because I was learning to rest and relax. Healing and recovery can take place only while you are in the parasympathetic nervous system, which means true rest and relaxation were needed.

When I want to solve an issue, I research people who have gone through the same thing and came out of it in the way I want to as well. So I found Dr. Joe Dispenza, a former chiropractor who was supposed to have had the Harrington rod surgery for his broken back following an accident he experienced on his bicycle while competing in a triathlon. He was hit by a bus and left with a broken back and in a wheelchair. He decided to not go ahead with the surgery, and he healed himself fully with his brain via meditation. I decided to immerse myself in his work. I did all his workshops and listened nonstop to his courses and videos, and I got heavily into his kind of meditation, which is pulling the mind, the stuck energy, out of the body. After studying under him for several years in-depth and having done all his work, I now meditate twice daily for a minimum of thirty minutes each session and usually an hour or more. I am eternally grateful for this work, this practice, and the benefits of meditation.

If being healthy and fit are always the goal, you have to do the work—and it is *always*, and it is never not a lot of work. I am always learning and working harder on myself than on my job. I am clear that I am my greatest investment, and the better informed and skilled I am, the better I get to be all around. I do not mean just in a personal development, mental, and business way but also in a healthy mind and body way as well. Work harder on yourself—mind, body, and spirit—than you do on anything else in your life. I always say the only relationship we ever need to work on is the one with ourselves, and then the rest are easy because we bring our best selves to them. We are the ones who generate the situation, and when we bring our best selves we create win-win outcomes.

I am always seeking the healthy, natural option and way, and the comeback is the hardest part. That is when you must make difficult, little decisions daily while in the company of yourself and no one else; and you need to keep pushing forward, never giving up. Champions are made when nobody is watching, one day at a time. Keep pushing. Always do and seek the next best or right thing, then the *next* best or right thing, and so forth. Chase what energizes you. Keep moving. Movement is medicine.

Take care of your body as it is the only place you have to live. Stay away from sugar as there is nothing beneficial to it. Boxers are clear that health and diet are of top priority. They know they could not stay in shape, be strong and fit, or make weight if it was not a top priority. Mike Tyson told me he thinks sugar is worse than AIDS. We all know AIDS is scary and deadly, yet sugar is disguised as sweet, fun, yummy, and wonderful but is the leading cause of many diseases and ailments in the body. It starts with "an apple a day keeps the doctor away." Health and diet are lifestyle components and everyday things. It is like brushing your teeth. We do it several times daily. If we only flossed the teeth we wanted to keep and forgot about the rest, we would have rotten teeth and empty spaces in our mouths. The most important word to pay attention to is *energy*. What matters is how it makes you feel.

The number one quality to possess is vitality, a way of thinking that is energetic, vibrant, alive, and filled with purpose. Choose your thoughts to get you there. Be healthy, live healthily, eat healthily, think healthily, and seek total wellness. High energy is infectious.

Have routines that serve you, stabilize you, and help you create balance in your life. I know what I need and I give it to myself, as being centered and balanced and feeling good and stable are super important to me. Therefore, I live accordingly. I have healthy morning and night routines that inspire and empower me. I wake up, meditate for thirty to ninety minutes, drink thirty-two ounces of warm lemon water, stretch, juice celery, and make teas that are amazing for immunity. Around noon I have a plain protein shake right after I work out and break my fast, as I do intermittent fasting. I prep my food, plan my meals, and am conscious of what goes in my body. I work out daily and know that
Health and diet are of top priority.

#98
TAKE RESPONSIBILITY

You can teach better by setting examples, than we do by explaining and talking about them.
— Cus D'Amato

The difference between us and animals is that we have the ability to reason and choose. And we are always choosing, so choose responsibly. Make great choices, and great things happen. When I own it, I can change it. When I am responsible, I am able to respond. That is a great space in which to be and exist. Every choice will either enhance your spirit or drain your spirit. One of my mantras that I often say to myself is, "I am the master of my fate, and the captain of my soul; I am responsible."

We all must take personal responsibility for everything that shows up for ourselves and our lives so that way we are empowered to know that we are able to respond. We must take responsibility for our thoughts, feelings, words, and actions as this is what creates our lives. We have the power to choose and change any of these things. Do not complain or make excuses because that does not move the needle. Instead, take responsibility, see how you can affect change for the better, and determine what you need to think, feel, and do instead. Earlier I mentioned my tattoo that says "Ho'oponopono," reflective of the Hawaiian practice of reconciliation and forgiveness. It is a prayer that says, "I'm sorry. Please forgive me. Thank you. I love you." To me it is the only prayer that is needed. It shows me that I am responsible, I am able to respond, and I *affect* change, and that is very empowering. You may not be able to change circumstances, seasons, or events, but you can change yourself, the way you perceive things, and the way things affect you and your life. If you suffer, it is because of you. If you feel blissful, it is because of you. Nobody else is responsible, only you and you alone. You are your hell and your heaven too. You are in charge of yourself. Being responsible essentially means "able to respond." So you want to be in control and take full responsibility for your life so that you can recreate parts that you love and avoid those you do not. Taking responsibility for oneself is an act of kindness.

You are the boss of yourself! You choose your own thoughts, *you* create your own habits, and *you* choose the actions you will and will not take. *Everything is a choice.* All the gods, all the heavens, all the hills, are within you. I always say that in any moment we can be Mother Teresa or Hitler. It is all about our choices. *Slow down* and know that *you* are responsible for how it all shows up for you. Create it the way you want it. See it the way you want it. Take actions toward manifesting what you want to see. *Visualize!* You create it all. Slow down enough and be present, yet ultraintentional, to deliver yourself and your words the way you want to receive them back. There is a distinction, a saying, in one of the communication courses in Landmark Education that says, "I create you, creating me, creating you." *I decide* how it will all *go! I deliver strategically* yet always come from a space of love and contribution. *I am the boss of myself!* And you are the boss of yourself! Govern accordingly.

Elevate your life by taking *responsibility* for who you are. *Become conscious.* You are here to create your own music, not someone else's. Do not die with your music still in you. The road to power is taking responsibility for your life, your success, your happiness, your choices, and your mind.

We must take responsibility for the space we hold here on this planet. Every thought I think that moves into action will come back because whatever we put out into our world comes right back to us. It is the Golden Rule on steroids. There is a flow. It is Newton's third law of motion, which states that for every action, or force, in nature, there is an equal and opposite reaction. What comes around goes around. Put out into the world what you want to receive back and *be the change.*

Being victims and making things and circumstances about someone else is the biggest mistake. It is one hundred percent-one hundred percent, not fifty-fifty. Just like the saying, "It takes two to tango," both parties are equally and fully responsible for what shows up for themselves and their lives. Our lives are mirror images of who we are and what we see. Wherever we go, *there we are.*

Boxers reflect on and notice their mistakes, and then they go back to training camp to become better and prevent those mistakes from happening again. They do not blame others for their performance; they take responsibility and are then empowered to grow from that and become the best they can be. The road to a championship involves taking responsibility for everything. People confuse *fault* with *responsibility.* The difference is personal empowerment. When we blame others, we

238

surrender control of the situation, yet when we take responsibility, we are empowered and create space for solutions to be found.

The most important aspect of taking responsibility for your life is acknowledging that your life is your responsibility. No one can live your life for you. You are in charge. No matter how hard you try to blame others for the events in your life, know that each event is a result of choices you made and are making.

Responsibility means being able to respond, not being the *effect* of something but being able to *affect* something. The quantum model is not about *cause and effect;* it's about *causing an effect.* Know the difference and

Take responsibility.

#99
FINISH STRONG

Only a man who knows what it is like to be defeated can reach down to the bottom of his soul and come up with the extra ounce of power it takes to win when the match is even.
— Muhammad Ali

Like a boxer, work until your brain forgets and your body remembers. Life is not about what happens. It is about how you react to what happens. So it is not about the setbacks; it is about the comebacks. Always make sure to finish fully and finish strong. Do not get lazy in the end. In boxing, it is not over until that final bell rings, and in life, it is not over until you stop breathing and die. Until then, keep pushing and never stop. Whatever you do and put your heart and soul into, or even just your mind into, finish it as well as you started it, if not even stronger and better. How you finish is mainly what people remember. It's just like when a fight is close, and a fighter loses by one point; people only remember who won the fight. The fight counts as a win on only one person's record, so it is not over until it is over. Boxers know they need to finish strong, fighting until the last second of the final bell's ringing. Really great and exciting fights come down to the very last second.

You are stronger than you think. You can always do better and perform better than you assume and think you can. Strong is the way. Know this! The destination is the journey, so be strong and

Finish strong.

#100
BE REFLECTIVE—
EVALUATE

I don't believe in losses, I believe in lessons.
— Alicia Napoleon

According to Bloom's taxonomy, a framework for educational achievement in which each level depends on the one below that is used to create effective learning objectives, evaluation is the highest level of learning. The key is to reflect, look back, and evaluate. Operate in the highest levels. Reflect and see what worked, what did not work, and what was missing so you can put it in next time and possibly make all the difference.

Being reflective and evaluating is accomplished through strategic questioning. Everyone has heard before, "Ask, and you shall receive." Everything hinges on the asking, the questions we ask ourselves and others. The answers are always in the questions. If we do not like our answers, we need to ask better questions. Change your questions and change your life. Ask yourself, *What do I want? What is the result I am wanting to achieve? How do I want things to look? Who do I need to be to have that happen?* Clarity is power. The language you use in your goal will define the way you receive it. When you get better, everything will get better for you. Do not worry so much about how you will do it; just *decide* you will do it and the answers will come. Welcome all experiences and stay in action.

An example of a question that would not move you forward is, "Why am I fat?" Your immediate mental answer may be, "Because I'm a fat pig." This is not a motivating, action-driven answer. A better question to ask yourself, for a better answer, would be, "What could I do differently than I am doing now to drop three pounds a week for two months?" Remember the acronym SMART, which helps people create smart goals: specific, measurable, attainable, relevant, and time-based. Ask yourself if what you did satisfied these criteria. If you are not getting your desired results, make sure to constantly repeat the process of reflecting on, and evaluating, what is working, what is not working, and what you can put in place to make it all that much better. Take time to evaluate and reflect on everything. Reflect on your day, on your interactions, on your plans, on how you will do things differently in the future, on what that will take, and on all you are grateful for and that works in your life.

Keep asking questions, be specific, and keep reformulating them until they bring you to the empowering answers. Be curious and follow your curiosity. Ask questions, seek answers, and continually work on getting better at asking better questions. Ask yourself two questions: *What do I stand for?* and *What do I want the outcome to be?* Bring yourself back to your *why,* as that is where the so-called motivation lives. We have a sign up in my gym that's visible when walking up the stairs that says, "When you feel like quitting, think of why you started." Who you are being is everything, and everything that shows up for you and your life is a *reflection* of who you are being. And who you are being is how you are feeling. Focus on the feeling and how you want to feel, and feel that way *now.* Make sure to get my next book, the companion journal book of questions that goes with each of these 101 rules to *reflect and evaluate* and to teach, train, guide, and motivate you to be the champion hero of your own life.

Boxers always reflect and watch the videos of their fights. They see what they did that worked and what did not. They then make adjustments accordingly in their training so they can come back better than before and not make the same mistakes. Making the same mistakes over and over again is the definition of insanity. Do not be insane. Be reflective and correct the mistakes so they do not keep happening.

Be reflective and evaluate.

#101
LEAVE A LEGACY

I want people to say that I fought for my rights. I fought for my people. I'm the most famous black man in the world. I'm a strong believer in God. If I die, I'm a legend.
— Muhammad Ali

You want to leave something; you really do. I mean, in the end, statues and all those things, that doesn't mean anything. Leave something we're all going to benefit from. I think that's what I'd like to do.
— George Foreman

People who do not find their greatness are irrelevant. A line in the movie *Braveheart* says, "Every man dies, but not every man lives." There is surviving, and there is living. Do not just survive; live the life you always dreamed of living. This is not a dress rehearsal; this is your one shot at life.

Champion boxers and living legends leave legacies. They live the life of a hero. Be like a boxer. Be your own hero. Leave a legacy. Be a legend. Be legendary. You are the hero you have been waiting for, so go out and be it. Be the hero in your own life, just like a boxer.

No one can write your story unless you give them the pen. Get addicted to becoming great and extraordinary. Wake up obsessed. I can do nothing for you but work on myself. You can do nothing for me but work on yourself. Work harder on *yourself* than you do on anything else. Be addicted to the process and to what is next for yourself and your life. The one thing you can bet on is yourself because you can control your choices and your actions. Know that you are your greatest investment, so invest fully in yourself, your expansion, and your growth. Ask yourself, *What do I want to be known for?* Your personality creates your personal reality. Think of the reputation you want to build, your top passions and strengths, and the group of people you most want to serve, and then build it with consistent consistency.

Leave a legacy.

CONCLUSION

Final Thoughts

Know that we all have good days and we all have bad days. Life is like the seasons. We go through winter, spring, summer, and fall like clockwork in our lives. Learn to ride the storms, plant in the winter, and reap in the spring. Reaping is reserved for the planters. Luck is for the prepared. Be kind to yourself and expect those good days and bad days, yet always stay the course to becoming the best version of yourself. Surrender, let go, make the good days by far outweigh the bad ones, and know how to allow yourself to *feel* however it is you are feeling. Then choose how you want to feel and feel that way instead. You are the one in control. Do not resist anything as that which we resist persists. Be the boss of yourself. Know that the hardest thing for a boxer is to be *on* when they decide to be and then to be *on* when the day of their fight comes. They train for that. They train to be *on* when they say so and to be optimal on the day of their fight, their performance, just as you can and now will do in life. Train yourself like a boxer. Live like a boxer. Create routines and habits that have you *on* when you need to be at your best, and then be able to turn *off* when time allows so you can recover. Find your balance. Be the energy you want to attract. The winners of history create history, so go create history and be the winner. Always seek and create the win-win. Chase your best self and be kind to yourself. Know that nothing matters, everything matters, and nothing means anything except the meaning you give it.

Consider these questions:

- What is the meaning of your life?
- What do you make everything mean?
- What do you value most?
- What does your future self look like and do?

- How will you need to behave?
- What new actions will you need to take?
- What new habits will you need to form?
- What habits do you need to quit?
- What new skills do you need to gain?
- When will you start?

Let these 101 rules be your guide.

Our only purpose in life is growth. Things that do not grow die. Grow yourself into the best of yourself. Just like my mission and brand for my gym, work harder, better, stronger, faster, and smarter for always. You, and only you, have the power to commit and decide to choose to be, do, and have anything you want for yourself and your life. Demand more from yourself. Do not just work hard; think hard. Be brave. Have courage. Love always. Live your life from truth, and you will survive everything, even death. People are afraid to die because they do not know *what is death*. The moment we know our *real* being, we are afraid of nothing, as we know we are a part of everything. Really get to *know yourself*. It is a lifetime journey. Create it, stay in constant action, surrender to it, and *in-joy* it. How could we truly expect to know others when we truly don't know ourselves. Fall in love with others, fall in love with yourself. Serve. *Connect to your heart. Feel and be love*, your true essence. We fear and stress over so much that mostly never even happens. Take the bull by the horns. You have one life; make it amazing every day—or not. The choice is yours. Be the champion of your story. Life is a learning experience; the only trouble is you take the test before you have learned the lessons.

Here in this book are all the rules to pass the tests so that when the lessons come, you are well prepared. People can often be their own worst enemies, but make it commonplace to be your own best friend. Champion yourself. Cheer for yourself. Be amazing and know it. Martial arts motivate you to explore difficult tasks, and then you learn an incredible amount about yourself. Meditate. Become more and more familiar with yourself. Get to know yourself. Work harder on yourself than you do on anything else, and you will be able to *bob and weave* and *stick and move* most effectively through life. Be the hero of your own movie. *What does the hero do? What inspires the hero? What is your highest and truest expression of yourself as a human being?* Life, or God, is speaking to you. Your life is always speaking to you. Listen. Pay attention. When the student is ready, the teacher appears. Let this book be your teacher, and your guide. Make sure to always go back and read these rules many times over, randomly, and intentionally. Embody the rules. *Be ready!* Boxers are strong, they fight, they never give up, and they groom themselves to be champions. Be the champion boxer of your own life. You are the hero you have been waiting for; be it now. Life is lived in the moment, moment by moment. Do not wait for it; generate it. Just keep getting better and better and chase your future, amazing self.

My vision is a world where people are self-empowered to take on their lives in such a way that honors themselves and the world around them. It is a world where people communicate effectively while coming from a place of love and serve as an extension of who they are. It is a world where everyone feels loved and knows his or her worth. The only relationship you need to work on is the one with yourself. Let me show you how great you are.

Let me inspire you to be in spirit. Fight for intentional transformation (FIT) from love. Allow your higher self to rule. The highest force in the universe is within you and all around you. Be connected to it. *Dig deep.* Do your own research, as in a world of information, ignorance is a choice, and you no longer need an expert to tell you anything. Become the expert for governing your life most efficiently and effectively. My intention is to teach, motivate, inspire, and wake people up to what is possible, how limited their thoughts are, and how limitless they can be. It is our beliefs that limit us. Let me be the mediator between you and your thoughts.

Remember and know this: wherever you go, there you are. Nobody is over "there" aside from the beliefs, thoughts, and perceptions in your head. Change the beliefs, thoughts, and perceptions in your head; change the sounds, flavors, colors, and pictures; and change your life.

As Wayne Dyer said, "When you change the way you look at things, the things you look at change."

Get real results! Make some changes.

Ask questions. Get answers. Create action steps.

Keep what works. Take out what does not work.

Put in place what you think would work to make it even better. Reflect. Edit accordingly. Repeat. Reflection and evaluation are the highest levels of learning. *Do them daily.*

Next comes the *companion journal* to this book, *Being the Champion of Your Own Life*. The companion book will take you through all 101 rules and help you master them through answering the questions. Fulfillment comes from wrestling with the great questions of life. The answers are in the questions. The clearer and more specific the questions are, the clearer and more specific the answers will be. Get ready to fight from love, to bob and weave and stick and move. *You are the champion boxer of your own life.* You are the hero you have always been waiting for. *You are it.* Be your future self now.

SOME PEOPLE FIND AN EXCUSE ... OTHERS FIND A WAY

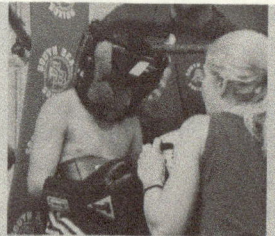

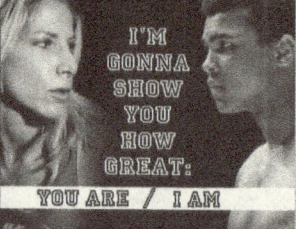

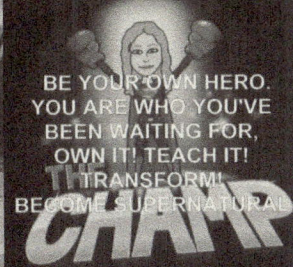

A BAD DAY
CAN BE MADE
BETTER
BY GOING
TO THE
GYM

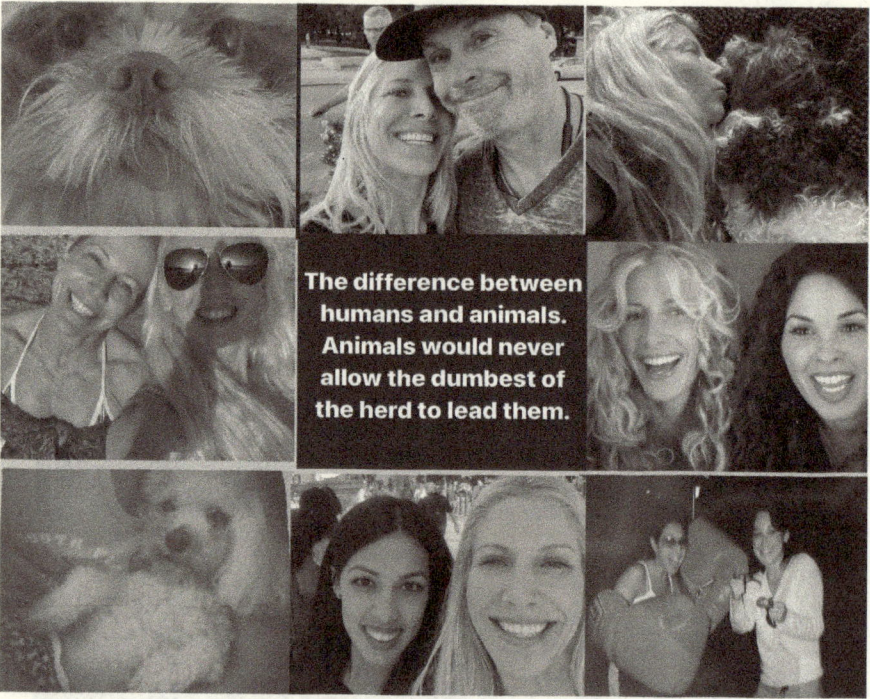

The difference between humans and animals. Animals would never allow the dumbest of the herd to lead them.

CONGRATULATIONS!

PEP
TRAINER
of the
YEAR
2020

JOLIE GLASSMAN

PLE FIND AN EXCUSE ... OTHE

BOXING
IS
MY
LIFE
FOREVER

"DON'T LET
COMPARISON
STEAL YOUR
JOY"

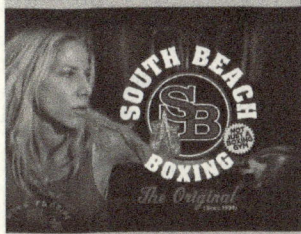

SOUTH BEACH
SB
BOXING
The Original

FALL IN LOVE
WITH THE
PROCESS OF
BECOMING
THE VERY BEST
VERSION OF
YOURSELF

I'M
GONNA
SHOW
YOU
HOW
GREAT:
YOU ARE / I AM

We're all in our own world
In one world 🌎
&
You're born alone
You die alone
AND
you are NEVER alone

MANIFESTATION
HAPPENS AT THE
SPEED OF
SURRENDER

FUN
FUN
EXPLOSIVE
EMPOWERING
INTENSE
ENERGIZING

I've got
99 PROBLEMS
AND
BOXING
Solves them all!

When you become the
HERD
Your unique self is
gone

ABOUT THE AUTHOR

Jolie Glassman earned a bachelor's degree in education and a master's degree in behavior modification in the early nineties and then her NLP Master Practitioner Licesense, and many other related, professional certifications throughout her career. She is a real talk, real results, teacher, mindset trainer, mentor, and coach with more than thirty years of experience in motivating, inspiring, and transforming tens of thousands of lives. Glassman has served as the owner and operator of South Beach Boxing since 1998, and it propelled her to fitness icon status as she has worked with many celebrity clients. She also has her own kids' charity called Jolie's Kids where she teaches kids to fight so they don't. She creates a safe place where all students can build character and find strength and success through the discipline of boxing and fitness.